D0152641

# RELIGION
## WITHOUT
## GOD

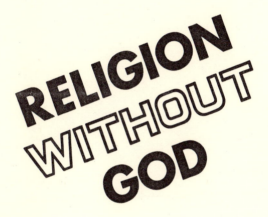

# RELIGION WITHOUT GOD

## by Konstantin Kolenda

**ℙ𝔹 *Prometheus Books***
Buffalo, N.Y. 14215

WILLIAM WOODS COLLEGE LIBRARY

Published 1976 by Prometheus Books
923 Kensington Avenue, Buffalo, New York 14215

Copyright © by Prometheus Books
All rights reserved

Library of Congress Catalog Card Number: 76-19349
ISBN 0-87975-073-1

Printed in the United States of America

BL
51
K65

63465

# Contents

# Preface

I celebrate myself, and sing myself,
And what I assume you shall assume,
For every atom belonging to me as good belongs to you.
—Walt Whitman


"Christians advance in Beirut." The year is not 1095, the beginning of the First Crusade. The precise date of the statement is December 15, 1975, and its source is the front-page headline in an American newspaper, not a musty folio in an ancient chronicle.

It is a tragic commentary on our time that in spite of

the realization that there is an essential equality among all the members of the human race, in spite of the great contribution made by the social sciences toward understanding, accepting, and appreciating the cultural diversity of human groups, in spite of a growing awareness of the mutual interdependence of all peoples of the globe, much bitter strife and warfare in many corners of the world are still caused, at least in part, by divisive religious allegiances. The notion of binding or holding together, one of the etymological roots of the word *religion*, remains as an ironic presence.

And yet, neither these opening remarks nor the title of the essay must be construed as announcing an attack on religion. The little word *without* in *Religion without God* should not be taken in a negative way. The thesis of this essay is that religion has a wider horizon than that captured by its traditional terminology, including, in Paul Tillich's expression, the tremendous word *God*.

It is not extravagant to suggest that the religious impulse and the questions raised by it are integral to the perennial human search for meaning. The fullness of life is an ideal vision to which a great many seers, thinkers, poets, and philosophers have contributed. We need to understand the particular nature of each contribution and to appreciate its essential thrust. It is often helpful to look behind and beyond the surface meaning of what is being proclaimed and to explore critically, yet sympathetically, the conceptual and emotional surroundings of a message. The arguments of this essay do not aim at discrediting the idea of God. On the contrary, an invitation is extended to see in that idea a manifestation of a desire to bring to the surface mankind's great and noble expectations from itself. These expectations are shared by all persons for whom the quest for meaning and goodness and decency is not a hopeless task. And this includes, I believe, even those who appear to be wholly at odds with one another when they militantly declare their parochial allegiances, whether they are of the theistic or atheistic sort.

The main objective of this essay, then, is not to destroy bridges between human beings but to build them. The underlying conviction expressed here is that there need not be any enmity between religion and humanism. Hinduism claims that it can accommodate and encompass the good in all religions. A generously conceived humanism may more successfully fulfill a modest yet vitally important promise— it may remind us that in spite of all differences in beliefs, traditions, and cultures, it is still possible to speak of the brotherhood and sisterhood of *all* human beings.

The frequently observed mutual hostility between humanism and religion is misplaced. What might bring them closer together is the realization that the quest for meaning is an open-ended affair. A religious believer without any doubts at all is in danger of falling into a sinful pride of intellect. A secular philosopher pondering the ultimate meaning of human existence hopelessly limits himself when he refuses to learn from religious texts. In their separate endeavors, both try to come to some conclusions about the meaning of life. They would do better to allow for the possibility that both philosophical wonderment and religious quest have a common source. They may discover that, despite differences in intellectual commitment, they are aiming at a realization of similar values. What each finally comes to accept in practice is not necessarily as divergent in basic intent from the other as it may at first seem.

This essay proceeds on the assumption that a dialogue

between a humanistic philosopher and a religious believer is possible and desirable. Both can engage in an enterprise traditionally known as philosophy of religion. This enterprise has a long history and a vast literature. The essay is meant to be a small addition to that literature—but with a difference. It is directed to the general reader or to the college student who wishes to examine the possibility of a common ground between realms that have been dichotomized into the secular and the sacred and who is uneasy about that dichotomy. Such a reader will therefore be prepared to make a new beginning and to start, so to speak, from scratch. It can be safely assumed, however, that a connection between the questions examined here and the traditional problems in the philosophy of religion will soon become evident.

This work is not an exercise in scholarship in the straightforward sense of the word; it enters no polemics and does not try to gore anyone's oxen. It may, nevertheless, stimulate a student of philosophy of religion or, for that matter, any person reflecting seriously on the meaning of life to approach this whole area of thought from a somewhat different direction. A reader familiar with the history of philosophy is likely to recognize many arguments and many echoes of ideas advanced by others in ancient or modern times. The essay is an exercise in what I shall call participation—making use, consciously or unconsciously, of a great repository of thoughts, observations, and conclusions that are part of our intellectual and spiritual heritage. To keep this in mind is to look with some skepticism on the importance of originality in this context. It is a common discovery by the student of ideas that a seemingly novel thought is in fact a version of a thought entertained in the past. Most of human wisdom consists in rediscovering what wise men have already known. The satisfaction lies not in thinking the unique and idiosyncratic but in recognizing that one is not alone in appreciating a truth. Of course, many a truth needs to be restated in a new way and to be put into the special context of one's time and place. It sometimes is rediscovered from an unexpected direction, thus becoming refreshed and possibly deepened. The result may be an inner peace. Such a peace, won in this way, may not pass all understanding, yet it nonetheless may be valuable precisely because it stems from understanding.

I wish to thank Rice University for granting me a sabbatical leave in 1973-74, when the first draft of this essay was written. That draft was read by Renford Bambrough, Bernard Williams, and Peter Winch, and I am grateful for their comments and criticisms. My colleagues at Rice, Lyle Angene, Baruch Brody, Robert Burch, Street Fulton, and Eva Thompson, have also been constructive and encouraging in their reactions and suggestions.

Last but not least, I wish to thank my students, Patricia Bellis, Bill Clancey, Marcus Wexler, and Eddie Zalta, with whom I had helpful discussions of this essay. Indeed, this essay is dedicated to them and to many other students I have taught at Rice for whom philosophy is not just a subject but also a source of delight. Over the years names and faces may become hazy, but the memory of such mind-engaging encounters lingers—they are the true and lasting rewards of teaching.

# CHAPTER 1

# Destiny

## Destiny and Death

Mortality presents human consciousness with an overwhelming problem. The central puzzle is this: How can consciousness come to terms with its own nonexistence? George Eliot reports in one of her letters a story sent to her by Professor Stowe, husband of the author of *Uncle Tom's Cabin*: "He heard a schoolmaster asking a little black girl the usual questions about creation—who made the earth, the sea, etc. At last came, 'And who made you?' Some deliberation was necessary, after which she said, 'Nobody, *I was so afore!*'"[1]

This simple story shows that the difficulty in conceiving oneself as nonexistent is not limited to sophisticated minds. The inability to solve this puzzle of the origin and destruction of human personality has contributed to the emergence of the life-death dialectic in its numerous guises. Each human life is seen as an incomplete term—and some reality is postulated as its counterpart. Life after death, reincarnation, salvation, immortality—all these are variants of the refusal to accept the fact of death. Because of this refusal, the life-death dialectic has become the dominant picture of human reality. Most religions deny the reality of human death. In some way or another the continuity of individual existence is affirmed—as spirit, as disembodied soul, as reincarnated being, as merging with the All.

All these conjectures are tenuous and ultimately unconvincing. They reveal something about the human consciousness, but they all try to deny the undeniable—the death of the individual. One should resist the appeal of these conjectures because the dialectic to which these conjectures cling rests on a wrong picture of human reality. We should ask ourselves whether this picture might not be replaced by a more convincing one.

There are people who accept the fact of death straightforwardly and calmly. For them there is only one life—the rest is silence. They claim that to treat the merely logical counterpart of life as if it were some other kind of reality—whether it is shadowy or spiritual or mysterious—is a delusion. They conjecture that we create this pseudodialectic for an understandable reason: to combat our fear of death. But fear of death is no more than love of life. (Goethe once remarked that death is a trick of life to have more life.) The impossibility of moving across the threshold is not ontological, rooted in the nature of things—it is simply a logical mistake. The very notion of death if conceived as a phenomenon is confused. For one thing, death is not an *event in life* because this event, unlike all other events in life, cannot be experienced by the person undergoing it; he is no longer there to experience its completion.

Perhaps there is another alternative. Perhaps we should agree with those who think our conception of life need not be saddled with the hopeless dialectic: life vs. some counterpart thereof. I believe that a better picture is given in the concept of destiny if the meaning of that concept is explored more fully from a certain direction.

The idea of destiny carries with it the notion of wholeness. What makes this notion applicable to life is precisely the fact of death. The inevitability of death may be the reason why some people are inclined to say, mistakenly, that the ultimate destiny of every man is to die. Mistakenly I say, because *the destiny of a man also includes all that he has experienced and will experience in life.* Human life as a destiny, as a totality, is captured more correctly in the religious picture of divine judgment, when a person stands before God and is appraised for the entire course of his or her life. Thus, one may see death as a necessary condition of having a destiny, of being a whole, a totality, that presumably, under some religious conceptions, may be judged for all eternity.

Malraux was not altogether wrong when he claimed in *La Condition Humaine* that "death transforms life into destiny." There may be even a germ of truth in Freud's postulate of a death wish. It is only natural for us to be curious to know what our life will consist of as a whole, what it will amount to, what it will eventually include. This curiosity may lead one to anticipate one's completion, one's possible epitaphs.

For this reason, growing older has its philosophical

compensations. To grow older is to move closer to achieving one's destiny, seeing one's life rounded out, becoming whole; it is to be open to thoughts, feelings, and experiences that are not likely to occur in earlier phases of life, when one is preoccupied with particular *fragments* of one's destiny and when the future appears laden with inexhaustible potentiality. Consequently, a consolation of old age may be a certain kind of wisdom, since one is closer to *knowing* one's destiny, better able to see *what it is* more completely.

When some philosophers urge man to think of himself as a being-unto-death, they call attention to the importance of this notion of wholeness. Thinking of myself as such a whole, I will not be preoccupied with reaching some further alternative state but shall, on the contrary, be concerned with treating every moment of my life as integrally belonging to this totality. At this point an aesthetic analogy seems appropriate: to see life steadily and to see it whole is to be interested in all of its comings and goings, in its interconnections, in its development over its entire course. Furthermore, one may recognize the importance of being concerned that one's life *has* a character, a style, that it exhibits a certain richness or variety, and that its variety and content satisfy one's values and objectives.

It is doubtful that the time of dying is the best context for answering the question of the meaning and value of living. Undoubtedly, facing imminent or inescapable death brings this question into prominence. Many literary works give testimony to the "majesty of death" by dwelling on its power to inspire deep thoughts and to bring insights into one's essential character, which may lead to radical reappraisals and even to drastic conversions. Tolstoy's *Death of Ivan Illych* is one of the best known examples of such a soul-searching instigated by the realization that one's life is coming to an end and that it has been essentially empty of real meaning. Joseph Conrad's *Heart of Darkness* gives us another example of a person who pronounces a verdict on his life at the moment of death. Kurtz does so by his exclamation, "The horror! The horror!" Marlow, the narrator, declares Kurtz's self-condemnation and self-revulsion a victory, a moral achievement. Interestingly enough, he gives another, contrasting description of facing the prospect of death, namely, his own:

> I have wrestled with death. It is the most unexciting contest you can imagine. It takes place in impalpable greyness, with nothing underfoot, with nothing around, without the great desire of victory, without the great fear of defeat, in a sickly atmosphere of tepid scepticism, without much belief in your own right, and still less in that of your adversary. If such is the ultimate wisdom, then life is a greater riddle than some of us think it to be.[2]

By giving us Marlow's version of confronting death, Conrad is implicitly questioning the idea that the moment of death *is* the best moment in which to pass a verdict on life. But even Marlow's version seems a bit too literary, too theatrical, too metaphysical. A less sweeping but more circumspect analysis may show that the period preceding death has its share of randomness, contingency, distraction. Only in rare cases will a dying person manifest concentration, inner peace, equanimity, and clearheaded acceptance. Ordinarily, he will reveal fear and anxiety. But whatever the person's state of mind at this extraordinary time, he can think of his situation only in terms of beliefs, convictions, and expectations that reflect his past experience and his previous thoughts about death.

What are the grounds for supposing that in such a

situation we will think more clearheadedly and with greater insight about central questions of concern to man? There are reasons to suspect that the elements of anxiety and confusion, inevitably present, are more likely to cloud our judgment. Are we likely to think about life more effectively, more clearheadedly, more realistically then? This is most doubtful, especially when we consider that efforts will be made—by the loved ones, by the physician—to ease the pain (often with tranquilizers or mind-clouding drugs) and to influence the patient's thoughts to encourage a one-sided, limited view of the rest of his or her life.

This softening and soothing ministry to the soul at the end of its journey is, of course, morally admirable; it is an application of the imperative to help each destiny experience as much goodness as possible. In this context, George Santayana's profound observation is worth remembering.

> To love things spiritually, that is to say, intelligently and disinterestedly, means to love the love in them, to worship the good they pursue, and to see them prophetically in their possible beauty. To love things as they are would be a mockery of things: a true lover must love them as they would wish to be. For nothing is quite happy as it is, and the first act of true sympathy must be to move with the object of love toward its happiness.[3]

Nevertheless, it is desirable to undermine the mystique that the crucial judgment about the meaning of life can come only at the *end* of one's life, as if in divine judgment. As we have noted, there are reasons for doubting that the conditions for arriving at a fair, correct, enlightening judgment are not likely to be present in these extraordinary circumstances. But the more important reason for needing to engage in a bit of demythologizing, or debunking, "the majesty" of death is that the homage to it may prevent us from recognizing that we are more likely to come to a balanced judgment about the meaning and value of life at *other* times, namely, when our estimate and verdict can be not only more truthful but also more useful.

It is an error to attribute a special importance to the verdict on life made at life's end. Appropriate and fitting occasions for pronouncing a judgment on the value of life are distributed across a person's whole lifetime, and the failure to make such judgments on those occasions is a serious loss. When do we have such occasions? They come at moments of heightened awareness, alertness, and aliveness, when we can fully and consciously appreciate the meaning of given experience, whatever its nature: interpersonal involvement—friendship, love; social recognition—in community, in politics; creative achievement—artistic, scientific; aesthetic contemplation—in music, in art. A life filled with such periodic affirmations is a life that *knows its own worth while being lived.*

All of us have our "red letter days" and peak experiences, anniversaries, celebrations, promotions, milestones, regenerations, new insights, and new beginnings. What we make of them and to what extent we appreciate their significance and contribution to our total destiny depends on our willingness to examine them and to give them their due. As Socrates reminded us, the "unexamined life is not worth living." To examine here means not only to scrutinize critically and censoriously but also to evaluate, appreciate, and, when the occasion justifies it, praise it. This steady attention to giving life its due, to acknowledging its worth, is healthier and more realistic than harboring a secret anxiety about the "ultimate verdict" made from a remote and dubious perspective. Much is to be gained from the realization that the meaning of our destinies does not reside outside the actual stream of events but *in* it, in the actual substance, the concrete content of our lives as they are lived.

Spinoza observed that a free man's thoughts are on life, not on death. There is a certain imbalance in lavishing all our attention on death, for there is also that other pole of human destiny, namely, birth. Not surprisingly, perhaps, birth and death always have been seen as fundamental events of human existence, but the negative appraisal of death has frequently led to a similarly negative verdict on human birth. Many wise, experienced, and disillusioned men proclaimed birth to be a kind of calamity. The greatest tragedy of man is that he is ever born, proclaimed Sophocles. In many philosophical and religious systems, coming into the world is seen as a demotion, a degradation; it is a fall, not an ascent. Undoubtedly, contemplation of the tragic side of life, of maimed and thwarted destinies, may explain the generation of such a mood.

But if the universe acquires meaning *through* human destinies, then every upsurge of consciousness through the birth of a person is a triumph and a privilege. It is a triumph for the universe and a privilege for the emerging individual. Every birth, as we also know when we are not gripped by the negative mood induced by a pessimistic philosophy or a world-denying religion, calls for a celebration. The vital, life-affirming instinct tells us that a human birth is a joyful event. The parents' concern is only about the new baby's survival and health, and the dominant hope projects the new person's continued well-being, fulfillment, and happiness. It is not improper to speak of birth as a miracle, as a victory for life—not over death, which is inevitable, but over nonlife, the barren silence of the world, devoid of significance bestowed upon it by a human consciousness. An experiment in thought should bring this point home.

Imagine the history of our planet differently from what it actually has been. After all, it is a contingent fact that Homo sapiens emerged on earth; a slightly different condition of our solar system, or even of some geological or meteorological events on the earth itself, would have made the emergence of human life, or even of all life, impossible. Instead, a string of fortunate cosmic circumstances led to the evolution of the human race. These circumstances were not inevitable and could have been otherwise. So if we value life, if we find it interesting, worthwhile, even precious and sacred, we ought to feel good that it has this opportunity to light up the cosmos with awareness, with knowledge, with the varied and seemingly inexhaustible projects of human cultures. Seen in this light, each human birth is a glorious event, for it is the starting point of a phenomenon that converts the dead, silent cosmos into a living, dramatic world. Resorting to an analogy with language, we may see each life as a statement to which birth provides the first letter and death furnishes the period. It allows the universe to speak out *what it can be,* as expressed in the unique personal career of each individual human destiny.

The concern with seeing one's life as a span from birth to death, as a destiny in development, calls attention to the interrelationship between the present and the past and between the present and the future. Consequently, it heightens the relevance of the concept of time to the concept of destiny. This topic requires a more detailed treatment of its own.

## Destiny and Time

Seen from the point of view of destiny, the three dimensions of time—past, present, and future—are abstractions. Indeed, this appears to be the case with regard to any significant event of human life. Time enters experience in all three dimensions "at once"; all three dimensions are relevant to every moment of time. It is extremely difficult to attach any plausible sense to the notion of a specious present or to point-instants. We see events and actions against the temporal background from which they flow and in anticipation of their effects on the future, whether immediate or remote. Memory and anticipation are not special states of consciousness; they are built into any normal consciousness. The moods of explicit reminiscence or meditation and the exercise of foresight or prediction are specialized types of consciousness, each reserved for special occasions taking place under appropriate conditions. In contrast, we understand daily occurrences, events, and actions as they relate to the past and the future. I see an event as a result of some other events or efforts, and I appreciate its significance partly in terms of what it will or is likely to lead to.

Occasionally we may dwell upon, approvingly or disapprovingly, what happened to us in the past. But equally well we may contemplate the future in a wishful, fearful, hopeful, or expectant mood. In each case we are seeing our present in the light of a remembered past and/or an anticipated future. In this respect human consciousness is quite fair and democratic; it gives equal attention to all three time dimensions. The accompanying emotions of a consciousness, whether positive or negative, are nourished by events in the past as well as by possible and sometimes inevitable occurrences in the future. As George Eliot put it (in the epigram to the first chapter of "Sunset and Sunrise," Book Eight of *Middlemarch*),

> Full souls are double mirrors, making still
> An endless vista of fair things before,
> Repeating things behind.

The carpe diem philosophies, in spite of their superficial appeal (because they are under the influence of a questionable conception of time), are bound to lead to disappointment. They simply are not realistic enough. Even the intense ecstasy of an individual moment is shot through with glimpses of the past and the future. All three dimensions pervade each instant of life. Thus time weds and welds me to my destiny. The carpe diem injunction is, of course, useful as a therapeutic device, applicable to special cases in which an opposite distortion has taken hold of a person's consciousness, that is, whenever either the past or the future has gained inordinate prominence. I may have special reasons for giving, consciously and purposely, an exclusive predominance to one of the temporal dimensions. Thus, I can make my past an exclusive object of my consciousness by a deliberate effort, as Marcel Proust did in *Remembrance of Things Past*. My entire consciousness may become filled with the past, with the detailed reproduction, reexamination, and resavoring of the previous stages of my destiny, beginning somewhere in early childhood and never penetrating the threshold of the present into anticipatory or forward-looking thought. The frequency of this phenomenon made Alexander Pushkin wonder whether memory is not the strongest faculty of the mind, charming everything in its power.

Proust's tour de force is a dramatic reminder that when I reflect on the meaning of my life, some past experiences may loom large and exert magnetic attraction. I may affirm my self and my world through reminiscence, by dwelling on and savoring episodes and relationships I have lived through. But this is possible only because destiny is a cumulative affair, and storing meaningful episodes and experiences requires the passage of time. My life takes on meaning and value as it is being filled out, as the treasury of my memory becomes richer. I cannot know the full extent of my happiness or unhappiness until the moment of death.

It would be a mistake, however, to ignore the counterpart of the backward look. Looking nostalgically into the past is but one form of savoring destiny. There are occasions, especially when in an energetic, enthusiastic, cheerful frame of mind, in which I welcome the surge of the future toward my present. This apparent reversal is quite understandable if I see my life in terms of destiny. Indeed, I may be anxious that time *does* pass into the future. I may feel the breeze of the future filling my lungs. In this way I welcome the opportunity for my destiny to unfold itself toward the future. Viewing my life as a destiny gives me a broad conceptual platform on which I can see my life as a whole.

When I allow the concept of destiny to occupy the center of my self-consciousness, I am in a position to escape, at least up to a point, the inevitable negative concomitant of consciousness, namely, the tendency of thought to break up experience into isolated fragments. Fragmentation is inevitable because all thought requires attention, focusing, definition, identification—picking an item out from its surrounding context. But the result may be a distortion, a staccato effect, a series of static forms or snapshots that do not connect into a flowing, continuous whole.

The realization of the essential three-dimensionality of time may help to correct this drawback of consciousness or at least to recognize that consciousness not only breaks up but also connects its objects. One practical consequence of this correction will be that even while thinking of some future event that looms large in my consciousness—either as eagerly anticipated or as dreadfully feared—I still will be alerted to its three-dimensionality. *When* it comes, it will fit into the triple scheme of past-present-future. This thought may realistically adjust my fears or expectations (as the Stoics rightly perceived, although for a different reason) by encouraging me to consider the larger destiny that envelops all my particular moments, past, present, or future. Consequently, I may see *each* moment of my life as a potential center from which all other events radiate toward the ultimate horizon of my destiny, fully encompassing the proximate, particular segments of my life's career, with which at any given time I am normally and naturally concerned.

Although time is three-dimensional, the present is not always *conditioned* by the past and the future. There are, of course, experiences that are not only conditioned but even fully determined by their past, for example, compulsive or habitual actions. Similarly, an action initiated from an explicit intention can be correctly described as resulting from or being determined by that intention. But there are experiences in which the present is fully open to either one or both of the two dimensions.

We can allow our psyche to roam freely in its past, in reminiscence, in daydreaming, or in a conscious attempt to recall bygone days. Such "fishing" in one's past has an element of sheer contingency; which particular images or recollections from my past will come to me depends on my present mood and on fortuitous associations. It is questionable whether the language of determination is appropriate here, for what floats up to the surface of my memory is not governed by my will or preestablished patterns; it simply happens. I try to recall certain specific incidents or stretches of my past, but I do not determine how well I remember. I simply must accept my ability or inability to remember as an empirical, contingent fact about myself. This situation differs from one in which the process *is* being directed or conditioned by unconscious motives or repressions. This is an important distinction. If we fail to recognize the distinction between the psyche's directed and spontaneous activities, we must accept the wooden dogma of universal psychic determinism. A thought or recollection should not be charged with guilt by association simply on the a priori grounds of a theoretical assumption. Much of what comes to our minds is innocent of harboring hidden connections; it simply pops up or bubbles up, with no strings attached.

Such spontaneously occurring thoughts or images may, however, *become* associated with some present or future possibility by an act of imagination. A *new* connection may arise, thus giving a novel significance to the way our experiences can connect. Much of novelists' or poets' creativity moves within this associability of free-floating memories and images with the themes or visions they want to explore. These themes or visions are usually not fully structured but are only tentatively formed or barely adumbrated, waiting for a stroke of luck that will connect the past with the future into a revealing or interesting insight.

The interconnectedness of the three time dimensions does not force our psychic life into constant goal orientation. As various unexpected items can float up from our past, so the unprejudiced observation and open frame of mind can present us with surprising thoughts, ideas, and images. Being open to experience also means allowing oneself to be surprised by its contingencies. Discovery is not always a consequence of effort; golden, or rotten, apples can fall into our laps. To close one's mind to such possibilities is, tautologically but not uninstructively, to be close-minded.

But even the openness of the present to the contingent contents of the past and of the future still presupposes the three-dimensionality of time. Consciousness is intrinsically temporal, hence three-dimensional. It is a constant shuttling to and fro, a connectedness of various strands and components of awareness. The object of a meditation, even a transcendental one, is not a dimensionless point. A beatific vision is pulsating and alive, even when it radiates peace and bliss. And to see a person face to face is to be aware of a soul ahead, within, and beyond the visual surface. It is doubtful that mystical experiences consist of staring at a static, immobile datum. Since the mystical vision gathers into itself the totality of value and meaning, it too must be alive, dramatic, vibrant. The flow of time may appear arrested, but within this apparent stasis dwells the throb of exhilarating fulfillment. The vision itself may seem motionless, but the soul of the seer certainly is not; it must feel and live through the motion of consummating its destiny. Such a living, dynamic tension cannot be one-dimensional.

Of course, in day-by-day living I need not and should not be concerned with my *total* destiny. Such concern is appropriate only in special moments. But it is desirable to train oneself to see time three-dimensionally, not as a succession of flat spaces or even of atomic, dimensionless points. The meaning of an experience arises out of its connection to the past and future. Only by holding all three aspects together and seeing their interconnections can we fully appreciate what is going on. The very phrase *going on* is here a helpful clue. An essential feature of consciousness is its "ongoingness," the dramatic interplay of happenings. Indeed, the prefix *con—with—*in *"con*sciousness" supplies a useful etymological clue. To be aware is to be *with* it, as modern slang puts it. A person who fully takes in what is going on has his wits about him, does not miss the significance of what has just gone by and what is coming. The present comes alive with significance in the light of this backward-forward reference.

It should be clear by now that the notion of destiny, as it is used here, is not associated with the notion of fate as externally, perhaps inevitably, imposed from the outside. The classical expression *amor fati* may be understood in a way that does not connote a sense of being doomed or oppressed by one's fate. It may be understood as the love of life, love of my life, my destiny, whatever its content. I may love myself as that unique expression that the universe experiences in me, *as* me, as my destiny. The sense of destiny as *moira*, nemesis, poignantly captured in ancient Greek tragedies realistically calls attention to the element of blind destruction of human values. But it focuses only on *some* possibilities for human destiny. The sense of tragedy is a valuational verdict on unintended destruction and undeserved suffering. To the extent that the universe as a whole does not guarantee the nonoccurrence of such destruction and suffering, the fateful view of destiny has a point and can function as a realistic reminder. Destruction and suffering are especially painful when they afflict young lives that do not have time to fulfill the normal desirable potentialities of human existence. It is this element of frustrated hopes and expectations that fills us with grief. One of the harshest situations to face is the prospect of having one's projects, desires, and hopes unfulfilled.

One thought may soften unkind blows of fate. Apart from consciously willful or ignorant human action or from unfortunate accident, no one is to blame for the workings of fate. The finiteness, the particularity of each destiny, always leaves open the possibility that on the large scene of human history some destinies may be cut short or seriously curtailed before they reach the full scope of their possibilities. It is incredibly difficult to accept this inevitable condition, but such an acceptance constitutes a kind of victory for truth, an affirmation in spite of tragedy. The ability to persevere in moments of despair and despondency may be enhanced if one is still able to acknowledge the positive content in the total sweep of one's destiny, although such content in moments of depression may be extremely difficult to retrieve.

There is some truth in the common view of destiny as something imposed from the outside, as something that happens to a person. I have not chosen to be born at a certain time, in a certain place, at this particular point of history. In that sense, I must "accept the universe." As I live my life, various elements are introduced into it by events around me: decisions of other people and happenings outside my control. Some of them are welcome, others are not. Some expand and enhance my experience, others shrink or limit it. Many are easily absorbed and dissolved into my life's projects; others leave more or less permanent marks—triumphs and achievements or injuries and scars. I need to develop a capacity to include such occurrences in my destiny and to readjust my view of it in the light of their impact. In one sense, I must learn how to become, up to a point, a spectator of my own destiny. I am obliged to take an attitude toward what becomes a part of me, either as a result of my own actions or of events generated by my surroundings. All of them are potentially grist for the mill of my memory, regrets, self-esteem, and future projects.

But even disillusionments and disappointments present an ambiguous challenge. They are not necessarily a loss or a liability, for they may plant the seeds of a more mature understanding. Many wise men have exalted the power of suffering to evoke from men their deepest and best resources. Suffering can cleanse and purify; by exposing our vulnerability it may also bring to light greater sensitivity and more tender feelings. Although initially painful and unwelcome, in retrospect it may appear as an opportunity to grow in strength and character. Both the painful and the pleasant occurrences, when made part of one's destiny and stored in one's memory and disposition, may become a more or less permanent personal endowment, giving a definite content to a person's self-understanding. In this way human life includes the transformation of outward occurrences into inward phenomena. Specific manifestations of the world are absorbed into a self, into a unique individual destiny.

## Destiny and Immortality

The idea of immortality wreaks conceptual havoc on the notion of human life as a whole, a destiny. Indeed, the very concept of immortality appears to rest on a misunderstanding of the nature of time. Time is inherently characterized by the triple dimension—past, present, future. The notion of immortality, on the other hand, appears to be wholly one-dimensional. (There is no news in heaven, complained William James.) To an immortal being both the past and the future lose their characteristic poignancy, and time is transformed into some sort of eternal present. The notion of immortality feeds on the idea of time and depends on conceptually lopping off two of its dimensions. Therefore, it is not surprising that we find it difficult to understand the relationship of immortality to time. Is it endless duration, or is it timelessness?

Less sophisticated believers in immortality tend to think of it as endless duration, as time going on and on. In doing so, they in fact return to the ordinary notion of time in which the future is recognized as an essential, and indeed the most prominent, dimension. The more philosophically circumspect advocates of immortality see this conceptual difficulty and prefer to conceive of immortality as timelessness, as being outside time. But it is not easy to conceive of the way in which timelessness is related to time. In this sense, the idea of immortality is nothing positive; timelessness appears to be no more than the logical negation of time and, hence, has no content of its own. Here the leap toward the wholly transcendent, that is, the totally incomprehensible and mysterious, appears the only way out and is the route usually taken, with uncertain consequences for intellectual conscience.

Picturing human life as destiny avoids this insoluble problem. Each human life is finite; it begins at birth and terminates at death. But each life is a particular destiny. This destiny lights up the universe from its point of view. Individual acts of my consciousness gather together— through my knowledge and through memory and anticipation—the possibilities and values available in the universe and open to me in my experience. Each act of such gathering is unique, indestructible, and "immortal" if we take, in imagination, the timeless standpoint of the universe as a whole. However, time with its three dimensions is possible only for a consciousness; hence, if we do not postulate the universe as a whole as a conscious force (which we have no reason to do), the assertion that each human destiny and each moment in it is immortal is but a figure of speech. Nevertheless, it is an appropriate figure of speech because, not being conscious, the universe is time*less*; it has no experience of time.

It may not be difficult to have a twinge of regret that the universe has no concern for time and, hence, no concern for timelessness or eternity. Nevertheless, this sense of regret evaporates when we look at the conclusion that follows from this realization. Because the universe has no experience of time, it derives meaning and value from human destinies. Only a temporal being can perceive the value of the universe as it is expressed uniquely and individually in each particular destiny. This positive thought will also show that the very idea of conquering death should not conjure up a thought of moving beyond life into some other mysterious realm. Instead, it should make clear to us that we conquer death in loving life.

Connected with the traditional religious conception of immortality is the notion of a transcendent realm—away and apart from the world. We are told that we must look for meaning *elsewhere,* in some other place, some other realm of being. But to focus on this realm is to distract our attention from the meaning and value of life. The result can only be a deprecation and depreciation of the meaning and value of the universe revealed in individual human destinies. For these reasons we should resist the tendency to deplore human finitude, to regard it as a ground for gloom and despair. Instead, we should think of finitude as a *positive* feature of reality. It bestows particularity, character, uniqueness, novelty, adventure on the world. Here Goethe's words "Nur in der Beschränkung zeigt sich der Meister" call for a metaphysical amplification. Destiny—a limited span of time—is a necessary condition of consciousness and, hence, of the realization of meaning and value.

One of the worries that gives rise to the question Does life have meaning? stems from the assumption that the world as a whole must be good, must have a justification apart from the goodness of individual destinies. This assumption, however, is never examined and, when it is examined, turns out to be without foundation. Indeed, the assumption is misguided; it confuses the issue by suggesting that a value judgment about the world can be made without a reference to a consciousness making such a judgment. The universe has value only for *valuers*. Unless we postulate centers of consciousness other than individual human destinies, questioning the world's goodness is meaningless. In the Judeo-Christian tradition the question is given sense by the declaration that God found the world good after creating it.

In the same way, each individual human consciousness can appraise and find the world good in the light of standards and values that it brings to bear on that judgment. Similarly, one can ask whether other, possibly nonhuman, consciousnesses find the world good. Animal lives, since they exhibit sentience, may bear witness to the goodness of the world in the sense that the world is animated by the experiences, pleasurable and painful, of living creatures. Such testimony of course lacks an explicitly judgmental verdict that only language-using, reflective animals can render. In that fuller sense, only human beings can *declare* the world to be good, to the extent that they find it supporting the attainment of values they affirm and cherish.

If we fully absorb this realization, we will no longer be haunted by the thought that some deeper mysteries escape us, that there is a Plan, a Design, and a Planner or Designer who, like ourselves, is looking at the world valuationally, pronouncing it at various intervals either a success or a failure. This realization may help us overcome the suspicion that by living out our destinies we are missing something, some intrinsically hidden absolute point of view that is forever beyond our ken. Such a postulation is empty, an unjustified extrapolation from the legitimate analogy that the world is as meaningful and good for countless others as it is for me. The meaning, the value, and the mystery of the universe exist in the heights and depths of experience that those destinies encounter in their cradle-to-the-grave existence. The rest is silence.

Nevertheless, the expression "the universe seeks meaning through individual destinies," even though not meant literally, is more than just a figure of speech. This phrase cannot be taken literally because, not being a center of consciousness, the universe cannot *seek* anything: it does not act as an entity in itself. But individual centers of consciousness can pronounce a verdict on the value and meaning of the universe by encountering value in their own destinies. Thus the question Does the universe have meaning? can be rightly replaced by the question Does the universe contain events and processes that by virtue of their value confer value on the universe as a whole? And since each center of consciousness arises in the midst of the world and is supported by its history and structure, both questions can be answered in the affirmative. This is the sense in which the universe seeks and has meaning. We can affirm this meaning without personalizing the universe, without resorting to animism, panpsychism, or pantheism.

There is another line of argument that supports the view that human life must be finite to have meaning. The argument relies on the analogy between the meaning of life and the meaning of a statement. The analogy is appropriate because in both contexts the word *meaning* is used, although this occurrence does not prove that the meaning of *meaning* is the same in both contexts. Nevertheless, we may compare one particular feature of the two uses and ask ourselves whether the presence of this feature is necessary for both contexts.

The feature I have in mind is completeness. We cannot say whether an incomplete statement is meaningful or not. As long as it has not come to a full stop we cannot say it is not nonsense. It may look as if it makes sense or is intelligible, but because we know that it is not complete or completable, we cannot *say* that it makes sense. It is possible that if continued further it would contain features, semantic or syntactical, that would make nonsense of it. For example, the incomplete phrase "The moon's other side furnishes . . . " could be completed in ways that would make it either meaningful or meaningless. It would be meaningful if it were completed by "possible surfaces for rocket landing," but it would be meaningless if it were followed by "square circle blik womble." If we are told that a statement is not completed, is not finite, but goes on indefinitely, we cannot say *what it is.* Consequently, we cannot determine whether it is meaningful or not.

By analogy, an infinite individual is not an individual because it is impossible to say *what he is.* Even God could not pronounce a verdict on the meaning of a life prolonged into infinity. As long as that life is still a *life*—not an unfolding of some preordained course—the person living that life has a degree of freedom of choice. A final verdict on

*63465*

WILLIAM WOODS COLLEGE LIBRARY

the meaning of that life cannot be made.

Each individual must be unique and unrepeatable. Furthermore, a life is a statement, a declaration of what the universe can be. Its valuational verdict is different in each case; every life is different from every other life. Thus finitude is a logical requirement for meaning. Otherwise a coherent statement cannot be *made*; meaning is forever in suspense, uncompleted and uncompletable. This is one reason why every human being can regard his or her personal identity as a unique and irreplaceable contribution to the meaning of the universe. Through this identity, this finite destiny, value breaks forth into the otherwise silent, inarticulate cosmos.

NOTES

[1]J. W. Cross, *The Life of George Eliot* (Boston: Houghton Mifflin Co., 1965), p. 499.

[2]Joseph Conrad, *Heart of Darkness* (New York: Washington Square Press, 1967), p. 112.

[3]George Santayana, "Ultimate Religion," in *Obiter Scripta*, (New York: Charles Scribner's Sons, 1936), pp. 292-93.

# CHAPTER 2

# Participation

## Myself and the World

If we reflect for a moment, we will realize that our ordinary perceptions already include an element of sharedness or participation. We participate in the experiences of others by characterizing and describing our common physical world. I know what others see or hear when I listen to their words or watch their reactions. In this respect it is quite proper to distinguish the human community from the communities of other animals, especially those whose sensory equipment is considerably different from ours. The perceptual world of chimpanzees probably is closer to ours than that of crabs and spiders. And it is safe to say that for entities entirely lacking sensory equipment the world is colorless, shapeless, and—since perception occurs in time—timeless!

Timelessness is a lack, an absence, a radical limitation. Without a sense of time—memory of the past, awareness of the present, and anticipation of the future—entities are deaf, blind, and inert. Nothing can *strike* them, nothing can happen *to* them, nothing exists *for* them. The emergence of perception is literally the birth, the dawning, of a world—its original genesis. Characteristically, perception is becoming aware *of* something. Something confronts me, stands over against me; it *exists*. Most likely, my awareness of self, of processes going on inside me, is a later step.

For an infant, experience begins with external objects, with the world; only later does it learn that it too is an entity within that world with a name of its own. Objects begin to mean something when the infant sees them side by side, compares or contrasts them, and pins down these distinctions by means of words or other symbols. Thus language becomes the orderer of experience and bestower of meaning. When the infant gives names and descriptions to colors, sounds, things, and events, its surroundings become *familiar*; they are recognized as being the same. The vehicles of meaning through which this sense of familiarity is maintained (or newness grasped) are supplied by language we acquire from other beings. *Their* speech makes it possible for *our* world to emerge. Herein lies the origin and basic core of participation.

Without its connections with its past and its future, the moment feels flat and meaningless: it lacks depth. This is true even at the level of ordinary perception. It is all too easy to fall into the habit of seeing one's perceptual field as a surface, where the figures in front of one's eyes are arrested, immobile. Up to a point, this may be inescapable. Perhaps it is the price we must pay for the presence of conceptual elements in perception. We give the objects in front of and around us a certain static character: tree, house, fence, wall. However, we can learn to recapture the sense of the three-dimensionality in our perceptual field when it slips away. If we succeed, the flat, lifeless world around us will pulsate with meaning. When this happens, space comes alive with active interrelationships, its geometric planes filled with movement, instead of being a dead receptacle of inert objects. Objects at a distance gain an air of familiarity and intimacy. The perceiver finds himself not only *in* the world but also *of* the world, an integral part and aspect of it.

The most common reason why the world is converted from a three-dimensional whole into an indifferent collection of flat surfaces is *distraction*. One looks at or moves through spaces without perceiving things in them, without participating in changes that spread before one's eyes. The distraction is often understandable. One is preoccupied with one's thoughts, following the twists and turns of inner mental life. There is nothing strange or regrettable about this phenomenon. The perceptual field should not always claim our attention, and it is a mark of a conceptualizing creature, such as man, that it can "turn off" its perceptual environment. Yet something is lost if one's senses are never allowed to penetrate the more inclusive environment as it unfolds its full scope and intrinsic character. This condition may be a most basic form of alienation; dwelling upon the episodes of inner life, a person loses contact with his home, his natural physical context. He becomes literally home*less*; his natural home is not a part of him, and he is not a part of it.

The external world becomes more intimate as we recognize how closely our perceptions are guided by our special human needs. The world in which we live is not the raw, uncultivated world. It is conditioned by the uses to which we want or can put the things and processes we encounter. Although I use the word *cultivated* in its original, primitive sense, derived from the Latin *agri-cola*—the man who works the fields to make them produce the crops he wants—the etymological "blossoming" of cultivation into the full-fledged meaning of *culture* is quite natural. Nature and culture are intimately intertwined in human experience, so intimately in fact that the distinction is often difficult to draw. Is it farfetched to suggest that language itself—transforming natural sounds into concept-bearing words—is the first phenomenon of culture? Named and described by human speech, physical objects and their properties are lifted out of the raw, literally nondescript, status and become potential items of communication and understanding.

But culture is a much richer phenomenon. No matter whether it began with the invention of language or of the first tools, the utility or instrumentality of things around us clearly dominates our consciousness. Apart from the rare intervals when, if we are fortunate, we are exposed to nature in its pristine state—sky, sea, meadow, forest—most of the time we are surrounded by man-made things intended to serve human needs, wants, and interests. More and more of uncultivated nature is requisitioned by man to do his bidding—often to the dismay of nature lovers and ecologists. When I look around me at any time of day or night, in any season, in almost any place, I see things, structures, and machines made with human purposes in mind. Apart from the clouds in the sky, an occasional tree on the ground, or a mountain below the wings of an airplane, there is hardly an item that does not impress me as something to be *used* by men. We live and move and have our being in this practical, instrumental world. Our world is thoroughly *civilized*, in the descriptive sense of the word. This world is our home, or at least our *house*, if the notion of home connotes more personal, intimate values. However, the house-home distinction calls attention to another way in which participation in the common world gives content to each human life.

## Myself and Mankind

Closer attention to the uses of language soon reveals that communication of perceptual features and of other factual descriptions is but a fraction of these uses. We are greatly interested to learn of the feelings, emotions, opinions, and attitudes of others and equally anxious to express our own. As children we learn that certain types of behavior are frowned upon or even punished by others and that some other types evoke encouragement, pleasure, and reward. In other words, among the earliest lessons we learn are the rules of desirable behavior. We also learn that such rules are maintained by human sanctions. Some ways of responding to experience, and some kinds of acting and reacting, are found to *matter*. People pay attention to them and resort to various ways of fostering the desirable forms and discouraging the undesirable ones. The manner of fostering or discouraging is most diverse and includes teaching, coaxing, praising, guiding, punishing, forbidding, excusing, persuading, pleading, and arguing—and many others besides. As a consequence, we constantly are aware of how our actions strike or are likely to strike others, and conversely, we react to the ways in which we are treated by others.

This whole dimension of human experience is encoded

in a great many rules, rituals, regulations, and principles that govern, or are intended to govern, our activities. There are various types of such practical guidelines; they comprise such separable dimensions as morality, law, politics, etiquette, and many others. These domains do not constitute watertight compartments. They often overlap or affect one another, but general distinctions can be drawn. Sometimes we criticize actions on moral grounds or respond to political ineptitude by casting an appropriate vote. Sometimes we merely remark on a breach of manners or on one's insensitivity to presenting a pleasing appearance. Occasionally the lines cross. A serious lapse of etiquette may have weighty political consequences, or a blatant disregard for the value of an aesthetic object may bring on a deserved moral censure. The relationships among the various domains of human regulations, of rituals and institutions that usually arise to support these regulations, constitute a complex and interesting network. Each domain may arouse our curiosity and become a subject of serious study.

What concerns me most at this stage is to point to these peculiarly human dimensions that so clearly dominate our lives in terms of objectives to be sought, practices to be followed or avoided, and values to be realized. Language embraces these dimensions not merely by allowing us to *formulate* the requisite rules and principles, sanctions, injunctions, and prohibitions but also by giving us specific ways of performing certain special acts, such as issuing requests and commands, making promises, delivering verdicts, expressing emotions, registering approval or disapproval, an engaging in a limitless variety of activities. None of these qualifies as a description or statement of fact—their linguistic functions are different. Recognizing and comprehending the great variety of things that language enables us to do provides a fuller, more realistic picture of what it means to have a mind, to be a human being, to engage in typically human activities.

When we participate in these various forms of acting and responding to the members of our particular social community, we do not draw on our own individual inner resources. We draw on the abilities, practices, and values that over the years have accumulated within the tradition of our community or culture. The nature, extent, and scope of these traditions are not uniform; each has its geographical locale and its history. At the same time, every one of us belongs to mankind, to the vast community of the human race, Homo sapiens. Our membership in this community is invoked when we are reminded that something is "humanly desirable" or, conversely, that some sort of act or practice is "inhuman."

In certain situations the mere fact of membership in the human community strikes us as important. A traveler, having lost his way in a strange, threatening country—in a desert, a forest, on high seas—welcomes the sight of another human being even if he does not speak his language and does not know his customs. Although he may also entertain fears that he could be mistreated, injured, or exploited, he nevertheless sees a stranger as a potential rescuer because he can establish with him a contact, albeit imperfect and halting, and mediate perhaps by some simple yet universally meaningful gestures and primitive expressions. He can hope that he will be *understood*. Such situations point to the kind of bond that persons cannot share with any other representatives of the animal species. This bond rests on the possibility of recognizing and protecting shared values, beginning with the protection of life and the satisfaction of basic needs.

The realization of this special bond should be supplemented by another sort of awareness, namely, the awareness of the particularity and individuality of each person. If each person is a unique destiny, I should impress on myself the thought that when I meet a person I meet a world. That world in most instances is a closed book to me; only a prolonged acquaintance and intimate contact can disclose what that world is. Nevertheless, if the values realized in human lives are the highest values we know of, then even *seeing* a person, a stranger on a street, puts me face to face with a manifestation of cosmic meaning. All I need to do is acknowledge with fairness and sympathy that here before me—hurrying, concentrating, playing, praying, reflecting, laughing, frowning, looking puzzled, worried, annoyed, preoccupied, angry, or cheerful—is a segment of the world. In many respects this world is similar to my own (since we share common surroundings, common human needs, and at least some aspects of our particular common culture) yet is a full, complete reality with its own unique destiny. Seeing a person is seeing a world in action, with its own inner drama, aspirations, frustrations, satisfactions, beliefs, opinions, convictions, and goals. Sometimes we catch glimpses of that drama in facial expressions, in snatches of overheard conversations, in actions and reactions of various sorts. The universal religious injunction to love one's neighbor or to acknowledge God's concern for *all* His children is a way of calling attention to the fact that each human life is a candle in the dark or, rather, that the light of meaning and value breaks through into the world in each human consciousness amidst its particular cultural setting.

The prosaic definition of man as a social animal takes on more weight, color, and substance when we supplement it by the notion of life as destiny. Personal interaction becomes an intersection of worlds. These lines intersect at many places, and these worlds overlap to a great degree. This is why two lovers in their ardor may feel that their souls have merged. Such sensations are rare and unstable, yet they present the upper limit of the closeness, intimacy, and the disappearance of alienation that all human beings seek. Actual life does exhibit approximations to this ideal, which poets and moralists recognize in celebrating the joys of love, of friendship, of familial devotions.

But even when we acknowledge the special character of such alliances, human worlds or destinies intersect on many different levels, to varied degrees, and for varied spans of time. Often they do not have the character of mutual support and goodwill. Instead they are marked by rivalry, competition, or antagonism. These, too, belong to the drama of life. Lives touch each other in many ways and with varying force. We see in other persons models or examples; we are impressed, repelled, encouraged, oppressed, hindered, aided; we seek and give comfort, inspiration, warnings, advice, opinion. The lives of others may touch us directly in a personal encounter or in community activities. They may come to us from stories and books, from real life or from fiction. Whether in shallow or in deep waters, we always swim in the sea of human experience, where each individual wave comprises a unique human destiny.

The sense of being a part of this immense ocean, of belonging to the whole human community, deepens when one reflects on the vast history of mankind. Each of us is a recipient of modes of acting, speaking, and thinking that reach deep into the past. In our day by day pursuits we may be aware only of the values, goals, purposes, and institutions that reflect the customs and traditions of our immediate group. But a little exercise of imagination can lead us further into the past when our grandparents and ancestors by their trials, errors, and experiments were transforming the circumstances of their times and places into forms that have become ours. Thus one may become aware of concrete links with other members of the human race who have prepared the emergence of our destinies by living out theirs. Seen from this perspective, my individual existence is a continuation, a development of a larger project, and I can see myself as its partial actualization. Although an individual in his own right, a child owes much to his parents and his family. This family ultimately includes the whole family of man, of which each one of us is an expression.

## Myself and History

When we begin to explore the connections each of us has with the past, reaching ultimately far into the recesses of all human history, we may be able to discover the deeper content of our personal existence. The awareness of the elements that went into our making, that helped determine our present general conditions and individual careers, *expands* rather than diminishes each human self. The greater this awareness and the stronger the sense of kinship with the rest of mankind, the stronger and the fuller is the self.

It is often thought that the contrast between the individual self and the vast sea of mankind must cause a sense of smallness, worthlessness, and insignificance. I am overwhelmed by the thought of masses of people who lived and died and whose bodies gradually dissolved in their graves. For a span of time, they inhabited the earth and now are no more. This fate awaits every one of us, goes the plaint. There are also everyday situations that vividly remind me of my insignificance among the vast masses of the living. Surrounded by a crowd of people at a train station, in a large meeting, at a concert or a congress, I may be struck by the smallness of my place and role. This sense of *de trop*, of being superfluous, is accentuated in the congestion of contemporary urban living, together with the anonymity of statistical, number-dominated, institutionally regulated human behavior. Much attention and concern is devoted nowadays to the malaise generated by the conditions of modern living.

But if we remind ourselves that in spite of being jostled by crowds each one of us (and each member of the crowd jostling us) is a conscious center through which the universe is manifesting itself, our mood can immediately shift from a sense of being a drop in the ocean to a sense of standing on a mountain top. The effort to find a right picture here is certainly worth making because the change of the picture may determine the mood and our attitude toward life. But the picture should not be arbitrary. It must be based on some plausible arguments.

We have seen such arguments in chapter 1. The key objective there was to organize our conception of human life around the notion of destiny. Instead of concentrating on the life-death contrast, we may think of the two contrasting terms as necessary conditions for the emergence and development of individual destinies. Instead of viewing the notion of time as three separable dimensions—past, present, and future—to which attention is shifted alternatively, we may see time as embracing all three dimensions at once. This view enables us to see each moment of life as gathering into itself, in different ways of course, both the past and the future. This way of understanding time will enable us also to see through the conceptual confusion associated with the notion of immortality; seeing that the concept is confused and does not point to any intelligible reality, we shall give up hankering after its will-of-the-wisp promise.

So when I feel overwhelmed by the masses, whether dead or alive, I should call up this picture of life as destiny. It will remind me that all the meaning and value that the universe *can* have is the meaning and value I am experiencing in its behalf (if one wishes to make use of this figure of speech), right here and now, at this point of the development of my destiny. This is all I need to do in order to reach the mountain top.

What the discussion in this chapter intends to secure, however, is that this process is not a narcissistic introspection, isolating me from the *context* in which I live my destiny. That context is all around me—whether I sit in a quiet garden or walk along a busy city street crowded with hurrying people. That context includes the immediate tasks and pursuits in which I am engaged. This realization enables me to go about my business with calm assurance, without being anxious that real action is somewhere else and not where I am. ("Do not be anxious about tomorrow," says the Scripture.)

One of the benefits of acquiring this new picture is that the hankering after other times or other places will leave me. All action, all reality, is for me right now where I am. This is where the universe, if you please, through my consciousness, *is*. So let me carry on, realizing the concrete possibilities of the given moment, keeping in mind that that moment is always an abstraction, with its past trailing behind it and its future beckoning.

Although on its peripheries my destiny is tied to the destiny of all mankind, it has a local habitation and a name, *my* name. Obviously those closest to me will dominate my attention because they are closer in time and space and are related to me in special ways. History has a wide horizon— a horizon that in today's world of global contacts and instant communication has stretched immensely—but its real stage, for each one of us, is a manageable circle. My knowledge, values, and goals have been given to me by my parents and by my local community. The scope of that community may vary, but on the whole it can be captured in a biographical sketch. In the case of more exceptional men it will call for a book or maybe several volumes. Some persons are so gifted or so placed as to exert an important influence on the course of events. Among them are inventors, artists, religious prophets, moral teachers, statesmen, political leaders, military heroes. But all men acquire knowledge, moral principles, political ambitions, artistic aspirations from their cultural surroundings.

The desire to reach a certain standing, a degree of power, success, or fame is normal and natural, especially when one's ambitions are sober and plans realistic. The interest in gaining the recognition of others, the desire to make an impact on the world and sometimes even to change it, bears witness to the fact of human participation in the drama of history. Indeed, the desire to make a contribution to that drama is a form of participation. To take part is to take an *active* part. The wish to enlarge one's destiny is but a counterpart and counterforce to the formative influence that the world has upon each one of us.

The universe seeks its fulfillment through many destinies: through each of us. Since there are many paths, there will be many experiments and failures. The drama of history, the way the world changes, is beyond the ken of any single observer and agent. Only in retrospect can a gifted historian discern the forces at work in any given epoch.

Evaluating contemporary events is fraught with even greater uncertainty. No one can estimate with assurance or predict confidently where and when significant changes—achievements or disasters—will occur. Apart from those few who guide the destinies of nations, large groups, and associations, all of us have strictly limited horizons. The lines of these horizons are not wholly stationary. In many cases, especially in times of great social and international mobility, these horizons may shift or grow dramatically. For instance, a person who emigrates to another hemisphere loses old allegiances and acquires new ones. Others suddenly awaken to their racial heritage. This also happens when education enlarges an individual's mind, evaporating ignorance and dissolving prejudices.

In these various ways of enlarging one's destiny (or sometimes seeing it enlarged or diminished by a lucky or unhappy circumstance), we are subject to the effects of those who pursue their destinies with greater intensity by utilizing special powers, gifts, and opportunities. This is the influence of the creator—the artist, writer, composer, inventor, scientist, statesman, ideologue. These persons transform their own destinies by acts of creation or discovery. But in doing so, they may also move the world with them. What is important in the context of this discussion is that the visions and creations of gifted individuals *are* capable of evoking a response in others who then become their audience, enthusiasts, followers, imitators, disciples.

We have here but another form of participation; individually achieved values can be shared. We often take part, even if only a limited part, in the creator's experience. When he plumbs his own possible depths, he usually cannot count on large audiences. Sometimes only a small minority of his audience understands and appreciates his creation or discovery. Yet such minorities often grow in size, and the individually attained value is shared more widely. This is how creators help mankind to develop its culture and to grow in knowledge, insight, and wisdom.

Participation in the experiences of others, especially when these experiences are on a high level of achievement, expands the human soul—it enlarges and enriches its destiny. It is, therefore, desirable and important to keep oneself open to such experiences, to "clean the windows of one's soul." Participation in the experience of others enhances our well-being and gives fuller scope to our intellectual and emotional life. A sound educational policy encourages communion with what is highest and best, with the minds of exceptionally gifted representatives of the human race. Such communion is possible. Each human destiny has an indefinite potential for spiritual growth, for taking interest in what is extraordinary or great, and for appreciating values discovered or created at other times and other places.

Our sympathy for the works of genius should not lead us to denigrate our normal daily contacts with fellow humans—members of our families, colleagues at work, friends in recreation. John Dewey once suggested that we amend the wise reminder of the Scriptures, "Sufficient unto the day is the evil thereof," by its obvious counterpart, "Sufficient unto the day is the good thereof." This was his way of bringing us back to the immediacy and concreteness of tasks and opportunities awaiting our attention and concern. Many of these concerns have a moral dimension; interpersonal transactions tend to engage not only our minds but also our emotions. Day by day and hour by hour our feelings shift and change, ranging from the sense of welcome and belonging to the moods of competition and conflict. Elation and disappointment, eagerness and melancholy, pleasure and pain, pride and guilt—all these and a wide spectrum of other states of mind invade and pervade our being. Naturally we are moved by personal, proximate, and local projects, and we react to and address one another in terms of moral values held in common. Those values also have a local habitation and local names—that much is certainly true about moral relativism. As everything else, moral values are acquired from the social setting in which they prevail.

However, when we address one another in moral language, when we can offer a moral *judgment*, we do emphasize that the locally learned principles that are the basis of that judgment are not merely ours. On the contrary, we appeal to them because we feel they deserve *universal* acceptance. Of course, we recognize that there are communities with differing, perhaps even opposing, principles. But we usually can explain moral diversity in terms of different conditions under which communities live. Should conditions change, there would be no justification in adhering to some principles. Furthermore, we credit those who now reject moral principles we take seriously with the capacity to recognize the validity of these principles, because we regard *all* human beings as capable of moving toward greater rationality and sounder morality. Nor do we exclude the possibility of abandoning some of *our* convictions when we are shown their faults or shortcomings. This is a way of saying that one of the objectives of morality is to move destiny—in oneself and in others—toward a jointly worked out conception of mutually acceptable ideals.

The occasions on which we think "globally" about moral issues are, of course, not very frequent for most of us. For the most part we are preoccupied, in William James's words, with the pinch of our individual destinies. This does not mean, however, that there are not people for whom the wider dimension of thinking and acting is a daily concern. Persons in positions of authority, charged with the tasks of keeping the world at peace, reducing actual and potential conflicts, and initiating a greater degree of cooperation and harmony, live on this scale. There are those who *must* speak across the barriers of local allegiances and parochial interests. If they did not do so, they would be shirking their responsibilities. They are rightly held responsible if they do less than *can* be done to promote peace, to eliminate hunger from the world, to reduce the pollution of our planet. Part of that responsibility accrues to the rest of us if we do nothing at all to keep an eye on those who are acting or failing to act on our behalf. Noblesse oblige is still a proper reminder to those with exceptional powers, talents, and privileges. In this sense and at least to that extent the future history of mankind is in our hands. There is no way to predict in what contexts and at what junctures of events the wise or courageous initiative of an individual may have national or global repercussions. Some of those repercussions may not be immediate and yet have important long-range effects. Nietzsche observed that great thoughts come on dove's feet. But which dove will turn out to be a harbinger of something vital and welcome is not easy to foretell— it may come from anywhere, from any corner of the globe. Consequently, it is fitting and proper to believe that the fate of mankind is intertwined with any and every human destiny.

CHAPTER 3

# Compensation

### Reality and Ideals

Religiousness is a complex phenomenon. It is not easy to bare its essential underlying structure. In looking for such a structure we need to consider some very general conditions of man. The first and perhaps the most important one has been mentioned already. It is the fact of mortality, finitude. The inevitability of death makes it possible to speak of individual destinies as *totalities*. This realization has its negative counterpoint. We meet an individual, watch its unique destiny unfold and then dissolve into nothingness. Or maybe our paths never cross. We see this other like a ship on the high seas emerge for a time and dissolve into the horizon. We realize that this is our lot as well. How is it possible that I, this particular consciousness with its unique career and history, can enter the scheme of things and then have to disappear from it, like the light of a snuffed-out candle? This question lies at the center of most religions, from the primitive notions of ghosts to the most sophisticated schemes of salvation and immortality.

The desire to escape finitude is dictated not only by the fear of death; it also prompts this purely conceptual question: What happens to *me* when I die? Because religions claim to provide answers to this question, they overcome the apparent stumbling block of total mystery about the disappearance of the human self. The answer, in most cases, is that the disappearance is an illusion and that some sort of continued existence is assured for the self. Unfortunately, when I press this thought further and make detailed inquiries into the nature of that continuity, the answers seldom are illuminating. In fact, they trail off into mystery. But even a mystery, some are inclined to say, is at least *something*—we don't *understand* the nature of the continuing, preserved, or saved self, but at least it is not obliterated, cut off absolutely, reduced to complete nothingness at the moment of death.

Because religion makes provision for this extension of the finite self into other, admittedly mysterious, regions, it can be regarded as providing a *compensation* for human finitude. The extension that religion provides compensates for the lack or void or absence that we feel when we reflect on the inevitable prospect of our total disappearance from the scheme of things. It is important to take a closer look at this tendency to reject finitude in favor of something else. The meaning of this tendency may become clearer when we examine more carefully what makes up that "something else."

One should be careful here not to make short shrift of this whole matter by latching on to *one* possible connotation of compensation. This notion can be interpreted negatively, or even cynically, when it is declared to be an infantile projection or merely wishful thinking. Compensation may be understood as already implying a futile self-deception. In this sense, a person who compensates for his deficiency indulges in unrealistic fantasies, closes his eyes to the actual state of affairs, and merely rationalizes. This certainly is one possible way of understanding compensation. But it is not the only one. It may be understood as a *positive reconstitution* of one's attitudes and projects in a way that *adds* to one's possible prospects and values. This sense of the compensation is quite common and can be applied usefully. Thus when a blind person develops a greater capacity for sensory receptivity of all the remaining senses, we can correctly describe him as having compensated for the loss of sight. Similarly, when a person loses one arm, he may develop a greater dexterity and muscular power in his other arm. These instances of compensation show how a limitation in one respect can lead a person to rechannel his attention and effort in another direction in order to make up for the loss or absence of ability caused by his limitation.

Still, a critic could object that analogies do not help us much when we move from a *particular* limitation to the *absolute* limitation, namely, finitude or mortality. What kind of compensation, what kind of remedy, is possible here? The objection has a point but is not necessarily fatal. We should remember that a blind man compensates for his blindness by enhancing the power of his other senses. By doing this he can live better *with* his blindness. Similarly, a person who sees his total situation in a religious way can live better *with* the fact of his finitude. So the question before us is whether or not we can make sense of compensation in a way that will dispel the sense of desolation that comes upon us when we reflect upon our inevitable mortality.

The path away from such a sense of desolation leads through the territory that we have already to some extent covered, namely, participation. We have seen that we derive much of the meaningfulness of our lives from the goals and ideals that were discovered, mapped out, suggested, or adumbrated by other human beings. When these ideals strike us as admirable and worthy of allegiance, we ourselves become their beneficiaries or champions or bearers. Our isolated individual destinies are enlarged, enriched, compensated for by such allegiances, identifications, and loyalties.

Participation in human affairs, however, is not a simple, effortless, unproblematic matter. At all stages, the question is always open whether, to what extent, or in what ways we are to join our individual destiny to the ongoing life around us. In more serious situations the discrepancy between actuality and potentiality, or between reality and ideals, is palpable and challenging. That discrepancy frequently is characterized by tension. For instance, we appeal to the principles of equal rights for all men and of the universal brotherhood of mankind, recognizing full well that many actions are performed daily, even by ourselves, that are contrary to the spirit of these ideals. Yet we still regard them as desirable visions. What is the status of such visions in our lives? Here, I believe, the notion of compensation can be illuminating. To make my own destiny fully acceptable to myself, I contrast it with the possibility of eliminating all of my deficiencies, drawbacks, and frustrations. In other words, I may compensate in thought, in imagination, for what I find myself to be. I may complete the actual with the ideal. I can try to fill out my destiny by eliminating from it—in thought and desire—all imperfections, whether they are imperfections in knowledge or in moral status or in aesthetic vision.

Compensation is the expression of the irresistible urge of each human destiny to see itself rounded out, completed, fulfilled. The upper limits of such completion and fulfillment trail off into the unknown; compensation is an open-ended ideal. Goethe's Faust realized this in the final moment of his life when he declared his highest achievement to consist of pledging all his creative powers to an unending ideal. This ideal is a "would be." The *coincidence* of the actual with the ideal would in fact amount to setting arbitrary limits to human aspiration. Those limits cannot be known to any man as long as he is capable of further thought and continued striving. He must forever compensate—in thought, imagination, and practical effort—for the limits set by his finitude and particularity. Interestingly enough, Goethe believed that this was sufficient to claim that Faust lived up to God's verdict of him as a good man, worthy of salvation.

Although his striving assumes titanic proportions, Faust can be seen as a representative of all humanity. Each of us seeks to compensate for the absence of perfection in our destinies and to move them a bit closer to what we would wish them to be. This can be stated more modestly by saying that compensation is the desire to come to terms with life. Again, this expression should not be taken in a negative sense as the tendency to resign onself to one's fate and to accept the universe and one's position in it without murmur or protest. Nor is it to be seen as a "realistic" admission that cards are stacked against me in the long run, that I cannot win, that the forces I must contend with are overwhelming, and that, at most, "life is a series of little victories on the road to ultimate defeat," as George Santayana put it.

Although some people would claim that this kind of compensation is a realistic stance, it is not the way we actually come to terms with life. This is not to say that we should insist on seeing a silver lining behind the clouds or, Pollyannalike, overlook the clouds altogether. But we come to terms with life only when we still can preserve the conviction that our shortcomings, disappointments, and failures do not add up to the *whole* picture of our life's meaning. To lose this conviction altogether is to be in danger of plunging into the mood of despondency whose limit is a catatonic state.

As long as a person *judges* his situation as wrong or bad or evil in some respect, he ordinarily does so against the background of at least a glimmer of the awareness of potential good. The sense of tragedy, for instance, is the sense of the *distance* between the actual and the desired. Because we expect from life the normal fulfillment of at least basic conditions of satisfaction and happiness, we are gripped by situations in which these conditions are frustrated and the fulfillment is denied. So ideals must be at work even in our sense of the tragic, and the phrase *at work* should not be taken, once more, merely as unrealistic wishful thinking, but as an active urge or impulse, a moral demand of the whole person. It is an active, not a passive, stance. It is a *committed* longing for the removal of suffering and an ardent desire to see the cruel actuality replaced with a benign possibility. Here, too, we see the phenomenon of compensation at work. Even when all the hopes and likelihood of averting doom are gone, the very perception of tragedy, of the contrast between the actual and the desirable, is genuine and redemptive because *both* polar terms—the actual and the ideal—actively and seriously engage the individual's judgment. With the withering away of the ideal, the perception of contrast disappears. And so does the tragedy. Only pathos remains.

It is not surprising that our moral heroes include those who have the inner strength not to break down spiritually under the strain of suffering. Suffering has been exalted by many thinkers and writers precisely because it is capable of bringing out the best in man: the ability to say yes to life, to the universe, in spite of tremendous suffering. The ability to bear calamity with equanimity and without falling into despair and cynicism is the deepest source of human dignity, perhaps not paralleled by any other kind of achievement. The righteous sufferer experiences and appreciates keenly the contrast between the "is" and the "ought." Yet he does not allow the cruel "is" to break him; his ideals and visions remain victorious. This is why such persons are honored as supreme examples of the ultimate reality of spiritual values.

Great tragedy and deep suffering, although no strangers to the human lot, do not characterize the more customary course of human life. But even in facing small frustrations and disappointments we can "bounce back," recover our balance, and renew our resources and determination to go on with our plans, goals, and projects because *we do not lose sight of desirable possibilities capable of realization.* We do not lose our courage to be. At every moment of my life my destiny is comprised of both what I perceive actually to be the case and how I compensate for it by rounding out the picture in imagination and aspiration.

Depending on circumstances, this rounding out may be primarily conative or primarily contemplative. By the former I supplement what I see with a practical commitment to some ideal or norm. The latter is an essentially valuational-reflective stance, when I am tacitly appraising the state of my well-being, or, to put it more pompously, when I ask myself whether at this moment I could affirm the universe and say that life, *my* life, is worth living.

Some example, even a mundane one, may be helpful at this point. Even when I am in a positive, happy mood, my mood may be disturbed by a simultaneous awareness of a discordant element. I am admiring the outline of St. Paul's cathedral while walking across the Waterloo Bridge, but my enjoyment is diminished by the sight of some ugly buildings surrounding it. This is a common experience. Seldom are we given opportunities to behold beauty unalloyed. But am I completely helpless, at the mercy of unpleasant facts? Not necessarily. I can restructure, in my imagination, the scene I am surveying so that the ugly elements are replaced by ones that blend and harmonize with the beauty actually there. I might even conjecture how the skyline might look were it actually fully designed and completed by Christopher Wren. In this way, the appearances may be saved; I can transform them to reinforce my vision of eventual possibilities. Thus, through compensation, I can round out my world, make it more full and more perfect. This imaginative reconstruction is a contribution I *can* make to my destiny. The fact that all of us wish to see the world as more beautiful than it is shows that, as manifest in us, the universe itself rounds out its reality by invoking ideals, *our* ideals.

Our example is taken from the realm of aesthetic imagination. Imagination, however, is but one form of compensation. Perhaps we can use the notion of *ideation* to cover not only aesthetic imagination but also many other ways of contrasting and complementing the actual with the ideal, including various models and visions for practical activity. Much of our ideation quite naturally and properly falls short of reaching out toward action, commitment, and engagement, but it may involve only our emotions and desires, lending a certain feel to what we experience and how we experience it, clothing the bare facts of our existence with a multicolored garb of images, wishes, and hopes. Consciousness is not a one-dimensional affair; it is neither thinly intellectual nor grossly behavioristic. Pure contemplation is one of its limits, brute reaction is another. Our actual exercise of the mind's powers may range anywhere between these limits, depending on the mood, stimulation, opportunity, or effort. We can train our minds to be more disciplined, thus acquiring intellectual competence, but we may also, with equal right and for the sake of legitimate benefits, let our minds drift along in daydreaming, wishful thinking, or sheer sensuous celebration. It nevertheless is useful to distinguish action-guiding ideals as a special form of ideation, because even our choice of giving full range to the play of imagination, to the expansion of our consciousness, should be governed by our ideal of the good life.

The main claim I wish to make is that *there is a capacity and a natural tendency toward compensation in each human destiny*. The notion of compensation is logically prior to the notion of completeness or perfection. Man judges himself by his own ideals, and his own condemnation of life is self-condemnation. What is important is that he is *capable* of such a judgment. Compensation in its various forms is the ability to be guided by ideals, to enjoy the fruits of contemplation and imagination, to aspire to a higher good, to face up squarely to suffering. Here, I believe, is the fount of religiousness. From this origin, a more thoroughly religious point of view may grow, infusing a person's life with a sense of purpose and aspiration. In religious terms, every person is an expression of meaning and value latent in the universe. Since each destiny is unique and irreducible, it reflects the universe from its point of view. We can express this even more radically by saying that as far as the disclosure of meaning and value is concerned, each destiny *is* a universe. Since every person has a capacity for compensation, and since compensation in its various forms is the key to religiousness, the religious impulse is not foreign to human nature. As a protophenomenon, it may seek to express itself even as opposition to a religion or to religions that have become dead, ossified, or burdened with limitations and constraints on further growth of the human spirit.

## Reality and God

Critics of religion claim that, contrary to the Christian belief, man was not made in God's image, but that instead God was made in man's image; the concept of God is a projection of man's ideals. The upshot of this claim is not obvious. It may be a way of deflating religion by treating the concept of God as a figment of man's imagination or as a wish fulfillment. But this is not the only alternative. The search for God indicates that the religious impulse is an important aspect of being human. That impulse testifies to the peculiar status of ideals. Although not actualities, they nevertheless betray an ineradicable impetus to endow the universe with a meaning that transcends individual destinies. Dostoyevsky realized this in his rather startling observation that the very idea of God does great credit to man. What is astonishing, said Dostoyevsky, is not that God should exist, but rather that such a noble idea should enter the head of such a despicable creature as man.

This observation mitigates the initial negative verdict about man's nature. Indeed, it does more than that—it almost reverses that verdict. Alongside of Sodom and Gomorrha there is a vision of the Madonna in the heart of man, an intense if often unacknowledged and unrealized desire to shed one's evil for the sake of good. When Satan says, "Evil, be my good," he must somehow rationalize that evil is the preferable or better alternative. Explanations for such a perverse inversion of values are not hard to come by; they usually involve a combination of ignorance, desperation, and self-deception.

The notion of God, it seems to me, is the limiting target of compensation. It encapsulates the desire to escape finitude, the search for realization of highest potentialities, the urge to translate ideals into actuality. God is the embodiment of perfection, but if compensation as the tendency toward perfection is logically prior to perfection, then the notion of compensation is a more primitive, more fundamental religious concept.

The traditional name for the unification of all the attributes of perfection is God: all-wise, all-good, all-powerful. One should not fail to recognize a purely intellectual, philosophical element in this ideal, even though other elements may tend to overshadow it. The concept of God answers the highest intellectual demands because He contains in Himself all knowledge and all truth. It is not surprising, therefore, that many philosophers were inclined to say that the quest for knowledge ends in Godlike knowledge. The notion of all-inclusiveness, of the absence of limitations, similarly satisfies the demand of the intellect not to leave anything outside of the mind's ken. God's mind is contrasted with man's precisely for that reason.

No matter how partial, each person uses this ideal vision to escape fragmentation and achieve some sort of integration. But the notion of integration is characteristically normative and open-ended. Just how much experience and what kind of experience would make my life really satisfying? This is an inescapable question for every one of us, no matter how halfhearted and blacksliding our attempt to answer it is. A Faustian man may be single-minded and heroic in setting his sights as high as possible and, as a result, suffer titanic anguish. I am proferring a more modest and realistic notion of compensation. In each destiny there is a desire to secure as much of life's possibilities as it is in our power to attain. Since every human being seeks such compensation, such rounding out of the actual with the ideal, according to his or her talents, insights, and abilities, it follows that in one important sense, every human being cannot help loving God if God is conceived of as the integration of highest ideals. This integration is not only theoretical or philosophical, but also involves the employment of poetic imagination, of moral vision and aspiration.

The idea of God is man's recognition of his own longing to take his highest ideals seriously. The very presence of this longing testifies to the reality of religiousness, of the religious impulse. Here we have, it appears, an analogue to what in theology is known as the ontological proof of God's existence. The argument runs roughly as follows. If we but recognize clearly what the concept of God signifies, we are bound to recognize that his nonexistence is inconceivable; God's essence implies his existence. Our argument here is similar, although it is moving in a wider conceptual territory. If the notion of compensation is essentially religious and if its presence is discoverable in all human lives, then the essence of religiousness implies its existence. The conception coincides with its own object.

There is one important difference between this proof, let us call it "superontological," and the orthodox ontological proof of the theologians. There is no need to assert the transcendence of God because we are led to postulate the existence of God as a transcendent being only when we inaccurately describe the religious impulse. Conceived in a certain way, religiousness invites a transcendent object when we interpret religiousness as a sense of distance between what we are and what we wish to be, or between the world as it is and as it could be, or as a vision of fully realized ideal possibilities. Because it seems natural to speak here of a *vision*, one is inevitably tempted to postulate an independent *object* of that vision, to separate that object from the vision itself and to see it as transcendent. When the Christian says that man was made in God's image or that man is God's creature, a carrier of the divine spark, he has already made such a separation. The same happens when another picture is invoked, namely, the picture of divine grace—that grace is available and within reach if only a man would reach out toward it.

Granted that in such theological pictures the transcendental leap has been already made, we must inquire into the ground from which it is made. The transcendental leap seems to be based on natural experience, namely, the experience of spiritual longing toward perfection, *away* from vices, from suffering, from confining and frustrating limitations. When that longing is strong enough—and it is very strong in moments of despondency or deep despair and, equally, in times of ecstasy or great joy—the moral and practical imagination of some gifted men reaches the superlatives of affirmation, thus giving rise to transcendent language. In time this language may crystallize into a full-fledged theology, brought about by a sustained effort to formulate and to formalize the highest reaches of human aspiration. While this phenomenon testifies to the persistence, ubiquity, near universality of religious feeling, it runs the danger of distorting the original feeling, of imposing on it a misleading conceptual garb. It may also be bent to nonreligious uses, such as the creation of questionable metaphysical pictures and the exertion of social and political control, establishing special castes of priests, of religious orders, and of church power, that affect all spheres of life. Under some circumstances religiousness may undergo transformations that make it into an opiate of the people.

However, to attack or reject religiousness on these grounds is to identify it with its distortions. The original phenomena of religiousness can be described in some other terms that do not require an object. If that is true, then doctrinal formulations may not necessarily lead in the direction of transcendental theology. We should ask ourselves what pictures or models or concepts would capture the phenomenon of religiousness without leading us in that direction.

We have one negative clue. The model of vision will not do—it is too closely tied to the notion of a transcendent object. Would some other perceptual model be more felicitous? Not likely. All sense perception presupposes an object perceived. We must look in another direction. Perhaps we should think of religiousness as *being in a certain state*: amazement, astonishment, wonder, well-being, fulfillment, satisfaction, assurance, security, safety, ecstasy, joy, and more. In sum, the manifestations of finding the world *good*, as God found it to be when he beheld it following the act of creation, are the symptoms of religiousness. Although triggered by specific events or encounters, the target of such states of mind is not particular events or encounters but the whole scheme of things that made these occurrences possible. Shakespeare's exclamation, "O brave new world that has such people in it!" need not be seen in Huxley's ironic sense. It may be generalized to call attention to the possibility and actuality of genuinely valuable experiences in the world. Rilke's speculations on the meaning of life come to mind:

> Are we, perhaps, here just for saying: House, Bridge, Fountain, Gate, Jug, Olive tree, Window,—possibly: Pillar, Tower? . . . but for saying, remember, oh, for such saying as never the things themselves hoped so intensely to be.
>
> *Duino Elegies*

As we have seen, the universe experiences itself through individual destinies. It celebrates itself in their intellectual, moral, and artistic achievements. Religiousness also lives in centers of consciousness, in individual destinies. A religious feeling may occur in an instant of participation, when we are struck or astonished by the beauty of nature or by the spectacular achievements of other persons. It also may well up from the inner resources in our own attentive and creative moments. In either case, we find ourselves in a heightened state of awareness and appreciation, and we declare the world—and our destiny in it— good.

Celebration, of course, has its counterpart: mourning. But mourning and its various concomitants—suffering, despondency, gloom—are states of a soul capable of appreciating the *loss* of what is being mourned. The depths of spiritual agony are proportionate to the heights of frustrated hopes. Even the devil, we are told, is a fallen angel. The claims made in the name of religion often emphasize its regenerative, redemptive power, but salvation, we should remember, is salvation from hell. The light shineth in the darkness, and the darkness overcometh it not.

Defining religiousness as states of affirmation, whether resulting from either superlative encounters or the conquest of our darkest moments, sidesteps the insuperable problem of transcendence brought on by the unhappy model of vision. At the same time it illustrates our "superontological" proof, namely, that the essence of religiousness implies its existence. This proof turns out to be a truism. Nonetheless, like other truisims defended in this essay, it is a revealing truism, leading us to see more clearly a centrally important dimension of our experience.

Religious belief is more than just an intellectual attitude. It does not seem sufficient to believe *that there is* an object corresponding to that belief. A religious believer is also expected to be related to that object in a certain way. The *belief that* must be supplemented by the *belief in*. Christians are asked to believe *in* God. That relationship is likened to an attitude of trust, reliance, and confidence—analogous to that expressed in the statement, "I believe in John," which really means, "I am convinced of John's integrity, honesty, and goodwill toward me." To believe in God is to trust him, to rely on his power, justice, goodness, and mercy. The linking of the two kinds of belief, namely, believing that God exists and believing in Him, is a function of the Christian conception of God as personal.

But if the target of religiousness is not an independent

being, the belief *in* that being, conceived along the lines of believing in a person, is not possible. Is the element of belief altogether irrelevant to religiousness? Not necessarily. The feeling of religiousness reflects a conviction that the scheme of things makes sense, is meaningful, and provides an indefinite range of positive phenomena that justify it. But the conviction that the world makes sense is a belief based on evidence. This evidence is provided by the very occurrence of phenomena found intrinsically satisfying. Thus it is not merely a matter of faith; it is a matter of knowledge. Our utterly satisfying high-level or peak experiences confirm the knowledge that the world provides suitable material for religious feeling. In other words, the essence of religiousness implies its own existence.

The natural religiousness of man is open to two dangers. It may be usurped by a theoretical tendency to transport the object of religious attitude away from real existence into a mysterious, supernatural, otherworldly, transcendent realm. Alternatively, it may be reduced to something less than it is; religion may be seen as a modest effort of the lonely individual to embellish his life by pursuing moral or aesthetic ideals, by lending his energies to the task of improving mankind, or by discerning in nature some beauty and design. These latter objectives are usually associated with narrower forms of humanism or with the liberal watering down of traditional religious faiths in which the believer ceases really to believe and views all religious pronouncements as only symbolic or metaphorical renderings of the more tender longings of the human heart.

This view of religion stands in contrast to both of these extremes while respecting the animus behind each. The assertion of the existence of a supernatural being is a way of bearing witness to the quest for ultimate meaning in each

human destiny and of seeing each destiny as a unique parti-
cipant in the career of the universe. We can and should
respect this affirmation without embracing the theoretical
conclusion of inconclusive arguments about the independent transcendent Being in whom this meaning is already
realized. We similarly can and should understand that the
pursuit of ideals is not an incidental embellishment, added
as a mere afterthought to man's physical, biological, existence. Man's search for the ideal manifests the all-inclusive
sense of worth and importance the universe discovers in
itself through human consciousness.

Thus, we should approach religion with the understanding that each destiny participates in its natural,
human, and historical surroundings. When generously conceived, this fact pushes the potentiality of each human
destiny to its highest or deepest possible limits. Translated
into concrete terms, this potentiality means that we have the
ability to appreciate the achievements of the human spirit
in its widest scope. This may include a proper homage to
explicitly religious leaders and prophets and a sympathetic
attention to the essential character of their visions.

Critics of religion make a mistake of separating the
message from the messengers. Consider a believer who
claims divinity for Jesus and affirms Him to be the Christ,
the Son of God. Here the important thing is that what Jesus
said and did struck His followers as extremely important, as
carrying a message that produced in them a deep response
and effected a transformation in their entire attitude
toward themselves, toward other human beings, and toward
the goals to be pursued in life. If we shift the emphasis from
the *content* of a believer's assertions to the *act* of making
assertions, we will realize that the factual historical claims
of religious language are not its most important aspect.

People respond to the example, the act of religious leaders urging them to change their lives. It is no accident that God is usually taken to be the embodiment of the believer's highest ethical aspirations. The tendency to address God as the Ruler of the universe in personal terms is a way of underscoring the reality of highest ethical values. *That* reality is quite rightly perceived in the lives of some actual human beings, who are subsequently given the status of messiah, prophet, and saint.

At this point we must recognize the irreducibility of unique individual personal identities and the limitation of the analogy between human lives and linguistic utterances. To be understood, an utterance must have a public, sharable, universally accessible meaning. A life, we have said, is particular, unique, and irreducible. But how can a *life* be understood?

In response to this question we may begin by noting that the idea of understanding has a family of related, intelligible applications. We can understand a straightforward, literal statement, and we can understand poetic utterances. The criteria for understanding each type of statement are not the same, and there are ways of teaching and learning how to understand poetry. To understand a religious attitude and to respond to it appropriately are more akin to understanding poetic utterances than to understanding literal statements. This is not to say that religion is just poetry. It is certainly more than a certain mood captured in felicitous language. It is a more inclusive attitude involving not only a certain way of seeing and interpreting the world but also of organizing one's commitments and moral values. It is not an accident that the spirit of religion is seen as shining forth in personal lives. Consequently, religiousness should include understanding in this broader sense of appreciating the unique, the individual. An appropriate response to a religious leader, a seer, or a prophet includes the acceptance and appreciation of his uniqueness.

There are, of course, universal, sharable features in a person's expression of his religious beliefs and attitudes, and these can be understood in the same way we understand straightforward factual or ethical utterances. There are no linguistic puzzles over the Sermon on the Mount or the Eithfold Path. But understanding and appreciating the person who manifests the *spirit* of these universally intelligible utterances is a very different matter. That understanding includes appreciation, admiration, approval, and perhaps even a strong desire to emulate the example set. An exceptional human individual, no less than an average person, can be understood and appreciated as a unique totality. The particular components of that totality may be intelligible in a literal, straightforward way, the way a literal statement is intelligible. But the conjunction of the beliefs, convictions, attitudes, commitments, and actions that make up a person's life must be understood in their particular individuality.

One of the important facts of religion is the ability of people to recognize, respect, and follow the paradigms of righteous, good, and ultimately satisfying living. If we look at these facts, we will be less inclined to ask rather fruitless questions, such as, "Is the believer right?" or "Does he have evidence for what he claims?" We would do better to ask: "Can we understand the believer?" "Can we see that the way of life he embraces as a result of his response to the religious message makes his life richer, more integral, more rewarding in terms of his ability to reach higher levels of sympathy, participation, and creative effort?" To leave such questions aside and instead to concentrate wholly on quasi-factual questions, such as "Does God exist?" is to leave the heart of religion and to concentrate on its thinly intellectual periphery. This does not mean that such theoretical questions are wholly irrelevant. Rather, they are secondary. They come from the core of religious ways of viewing experience. The reality of God is affirmed in the Godlike, spiritually superior lives of especially gifted persons and in the ability of other human beings to be moved and even profoundly changed by such lives. These are the *relevant* facts of religion.

One of the stumbling blocks of religion is the hard and fast dichotomy between the profane and the sacred. "Sunday religion" is one of the effects of such dichotomizing. Actual daily life is much more generous with opportunities for the encounter with values that point in the direction of religious experience. The very notion of value carries with it a claim on our attention. To say that something has value or is valuable is to invite participation in it. There is a difference between declaring that I like something and saying that it is good. The latter is an objective claim. I may like something without claiming that it is good. Indeed, I may confess to liking something knowing full well that it is not worth much. The situation is different when we are inclined to call something good or valuable. When we do so, we are saying that others are likely to find in it something good as well, that its value is objective.

We can enrich our vocabulary while dealing with this point. The term I wish to introduce is the one St. Thomas Aquinas used to characterize beautiful objects. He spoke of them as having *radiance*. Radiance is the capacity of something—object, event, act, or process—to attract attention to itself. Radiance accompanies participation. We are attracted to some features of both nature and man. Paying attention to them, and sometimes being absorbed in them, makes our lives deeper, wiser, better, more thrilling, and more satisfying. All sorts of phenomena, on an indefinite scale of value and attractiveness, can manifest radiance.

Examples of radiance are all around us. When we are moved by music, by a spoken word, by a display of intellectual power, by an admirable deed, a skillful performance, an ingenious invention, by a winning smile, or a generous impulse, we are exposed to their radiance. Their very character is such that it is a loss for us to miss them. If we fail to respond to them, we impoverish our destiny, especially when we waste our attention on something less interesting or less worthy or, even worse, when we dissipate it altogether. Our response to other persons, living or dead, is not merely intellectual. In George Eliot's words, "ideas are often poor ghosts . . . they pass athwart us in thin vapour and cannot make themselves felt." But we do not always respond to ideas in their disembodied state. They strike us, make an impression on us when they are embodied in other people's experience or when, as Eliot states, they are made flesh. In such situations they "speak to us in appealing tones; they are clothed in a human soul, with all its conflicts, its faith. . . . Then their presence is power . . . and we are drawn after them with gentle compulsion."[1] There may be no better statement of what I mean by participation.

Most religions champion love of one's fellow man, but this injunction is often overshadowed by a concern for personal salvation. Although in one sense each destiny seeks its own fulfillment or salvation, it may show a narcissistic bias. When this bias is the more pronounced, less attention is given to the way each destiny is open to enrichment by other destinies. A positive feature of one's finitude may be a selfless admiration for the values realized in the lives of others.

A capacity for identification with the attainments and experiences of others may be a better alternative to the constant effort of dwelling on what one can bring about by oneself. Having tried to become a musician, a poet, a scientist, or a philosopher and having realized how difficult it is to produce a new composition, a fresh image, a novel theory, or an original thought, one may be genuinely pleased, impressed, even astonished by seeing someone else produce something new and good. An encounter with novel, radiating experiences may help to create a sense of kinship, of true participation in the discoveries and achievements of others. Such an experience, because it is wholly other-directed and purely objective, carries with it the possibility of being surprised by pure joy and perfect peace. Radiance speaks: behold how wonderful *human beings* can be! It is not surprising that at such moments life as a whole and the entire universe should appear as if lit up by the human spirit.

There is of course a need to be prepared to receive such experiences, which is another argument for general education. The capacity for objective sympathy with various forms of radiance will be the more genuine the more we can understand the quality and character of the shared experience. To the extent that we can follow a great insight, a poetic flight, an ingenious theory, a skillful performance, we come to appreciate the possibilities open to others and to grow with them ourselves.

A rich, well-rounded life is still our ideal, and a life wasted on trivialities fills us with regret. Failing to reach out toward the more difficult and the more demanding is a mark of laziness or inertia (it is easy to be well-rounded when one's radius is short). Well-roundedness necessitates a willingness to participate in a great many kinds of activities and experiences. The more understanding, sympathetic, and sophisticated that participation is, the more interesting and rewarding a given life is. There is no need to jump to aristocratic or elitist conclusions. Those who "take in" more of mankind's discoveries, achievements, and enthusiasms because of connections, or talent, or accident of birth are fortunate and privileged. But it is nevertheless true that, barring the extremes of poverty or ill health, the core of humanly rewarding experiences is open to everyone. All of us "repeat" the discoveries made for us by others—in the storehouse of language, manners, conventions, and rituals, among the treasures of knowledge and of practical inventions. All of us live on capital provided by our fellow men. Sometimes we can stand on the shoulders of giants.

As useful as the metaphor of capital may be, it does have limitations we should not overlook. Indeed, we should remember that economics has been called "the dismal science." The notion of capital is in some ways quite inappropriate here. Capital is the counterpart of scarcity; it is in constant danger of being *used* up. This does not happen to the values transmitted to others. Cultural capital does not diminish in the process of transmission; on the contrary, it increases. Cultural commodities have their being only when they are used. When the living absorb inherited cultural values, they are not taking them away from the dead. The creators of such values enrich their own lives in the very acts of creation, but once created, these values can be used again and again by others who re-create them and relive them in their own experience. The fact that human discoveries and achievements have this built-in, indefinite fecundity may explain the univeral human desire to leave something to posterity—a meaningful object, a thought, or an artifact. This desire is not necessarily vain or unrealistic; it has its basis in the sharable nature of human experience. Much of what we discover and cherish can be rediscovered and cherished by others.

Consider Keat's sonnet "When I Have Fears":

When I have fears that I may cease to be
   Before my pen has glean'd my teeming brain,
Before high piled books, in charactry,
   Hold like rich garners the full-ripen'd grain;
When I behold, upon the night's starr'd face,
   Huge cloudy symbols of a high romance,
And think that I may never live to trace
   Their shadows, with the magic hand of chance;
And when I feel, fair creature of an hour!
   That I shall never look upon thee more,
Never have relish in the faery power
   Of unreflecting love;—then on the shore
Of the wide world I stand alone, and think
   Till Love and Fame to nothingness do sink.

What does it mean to appreciate this poem if we know that Keats is dead? It is to enter into the quality of the experience he himself had and captured in this poem. We almost literally try to repeat that experience, to make it live again, an act that would be impossible if Keats had not had this experience or had not expressed it in this way. Of course, there is no comfort in this for Keats—a logical truth, for Keats is no more—but there *is* comfort and value for everyone who can see and feel more than he otherwise would have been able to if Keats had never existed.

The phenomena we are discussing are not supernatural or otherworldly; they happen in time and in particular human careers. Yet they are the materials for a religious attitude toward one's destiny and toward the destiny of mankind. Things that constitute the flesh and blood of religion are the phenomena of love, aspiration, the urge toward perfection—moral and artistic and scientific. Thus the lives of saints, moral heroes, artistic geniuses, intellectual discoverers, benefactors of mankind (statesmen, scientists, engineers, inventors, ecologists) are the proper subjects for the investigation of the possibilities for participation, radiance, and religion.

The secrets of the universe are stored in the ongoing experience of mankind, in the careers of all human destinies. Rather than seeking the key to these secrets in such shortcuts as empty mystical visions or occult manifestations, we should look for it in the longings and achievements of actual persons, living or dead—in all dimensions of the human spirit. But we need not neglect or ignore the spiritual nourishment available in daily experience, in the arena of our familiar pursuits. My life, my destiny, is where I am, and I should seize the opportunity to respond to radiance around me and to "brighten the corner" where I am. I rob myself when I fail to respond to the beauty around me, whether it is in nature or in the man-made world. I rob others when I fail to use talents that could provide satisfying experiences for them. In either way, my destiny is impoverished—and so is the universe. A religious attitude will not be indifferent to this loss.

## Reality and Evil

The view of religion developed in this essay is not saddled with the thorny problem of evil. Although the presence of evil in the world has provided a fertile ground for the growth of religious consciousness and the notion of evil may have its full force only in the context of religious language, theological accounts of the origin and nature of evil often

have furnished a decisive stumbling block for many believers and would-be believers. The problem is inescapable
for a view that postulates the existence of a Supreme Being
who created and rules the universe. That Being is at the
same time all-good and all-powerful. But the palpable presence of evil in the world is incompatible with the copresence
of these attributes in God. Theology has struggled, incon-
clusively, to say the least, with the task of reconciling this
inner rift at the heart of traditional religion.

The theoretical problem disappears as soon as the
notion of a separate, transcendent Being—with His own
consciousness, designs, and dispositions—is abandoned. To
say, however, that the *problem* disappears is not to say that
*evil* does. The evil remains, but not as a problem. On the
contrary, it loses its mystique and mystery. It can be iden-
tified, named. With that knowledge may come a clearheaded recognition of the forms it takes, of the reasons why
it should be combated whenever possible, and of the means
by which this can be done effectively. There may be moral
gains in demythologizing the concept of evil.

Brooding upon the unavoidable and often unforesee-
able blows of misfortune and undeserved suffering, the
injured human psyche tends to personify evil, to ascribe it
to a demonic agency, the Evil One, the Devil. But this per-
sonification of evil, although an understandable poetic-
mythical response to suffering and tragedy, is based on a
mistake. The devil does not exist; he is a papier-mâché
Mephistopheles. To represent "him" as an enemy is to dig-
nify evil by elevating it to the status of an intelligent, moti-
vated agency. A mature wisdom would refuse the devil any
standing in the realm of meaning, which is applicable only
to conscious beings. In the prologue to *Faust*, Goethe
observed that evil is inherently inferior in the world which,

insofar as it is divinely ordered, seeks to promote life and its values. In the quest for meaning and value, evil as personified force does not exist; it is not an independently acting obstacle. This realization prompted Socrates to declare that no real evil can befall a good man; such a man is absolutely safe. This does not mean that evil does not *happen*. In spite of all luck and good fortune, no one can escape some evil actions, events, or consequences. But the first step toward compensating for misfortune, toward taking it up realistically into one's destiny, is to recognize clearly its inert nature: it is indifferent to what we seek, to what the universe *in us* seeks. Evil is either a blind, nonmoral force or, alternatively, the work of sick, distorted, and often pitiable men. When we are consciously doing evil to others, we are destroying the good in ourselves as well.

Evil manifests itself as the negation of the three ultimate values defended in this essay: destiny, participation, and compensation. These forms of moral evil should be distinguished from the nonmoral forms. We speak of evil consequences due to natural causes: earthquakes, floods, fires, diseases. Undoubtedly we can rightly say that death or suffering inflicted by such causes is evil, but natural events are themselves evil only in an animistic sense. Part of the *problem* of evil for a traditional believer lies in the way he regards nature. Since all phenomena in nature ultimately are governed by God's will, such afflictions are either deserved punishments or the result of some roundabout, implausible explanation, such as the mysteriousness of the ways in which God moves. Thus an innocent victim's death in an avalanche is ascribed to God's unfathomable wisdom. But natural phenomena are neither good nor bad in themselves and cannot be regarded as manifestations of evil. The full force of the word *evil* is at work when an intent is discernible or when the agency responsible for evil is at least capable of modifying its intentions and actions. Subsequent discussion will deal with evil in its full, moral sense.

## *Evil and Destiny*

Of all the words in our moral vocabulary the word *murder* is probably most heavily laden with condemnation. Its emotive charge is even stronger than that of the verb *to kill.* Why should this be so? A murder, an intentional killing, is a negation of a destiny. In killing a person, we are killing a world. This explains the deep sense of loss that follows a discovery that a life has been terminated. When a human being is destroyed, the universe loses a window through which it consciously experiences, enjoys, and learns about itself. This loss normally strikes surrounding lives as something terrible and tragic. Death emanates its own dark, disconsolate radiance. The universe mourns the demise of a unique, irreplaceable expression of itself.

The conclusion that what is being mourned is the destruction, the denial, of a destiny is reinforced in the face of *untimely* death, when the destiny of a person is still fully ahead of him, unlived, unexperienced, unfulfilled. By the same token, a death that terminates a normal full span of life does not usually have such an intense effect of desolation. Indeed, when we recall that death is an integral part of each human destiny, provided it comes at a right time—in the ripeness of years, with a lifetime of activity in its store, and with influences and memories around it—we can see that such a death is not evil. It does not come as an enemy, neither to the person himself nor to the survivors. The radiance of mourning for such a deceased, especially if the life was good, creative, and happy, may be suffused with a sense of fulfillment, acceptance, and admiration. To have lived a good life, to die without excessive discomfort or pain, without inflicting too many burdens on others, is a "consummation devoutly to be wished."

Most of us consider a person who can commit premeditated, cold-blooded murder as the most terrifying sort of being. There is something frightening about the very thought of such a person; he appears completely inhuman, oblivious to the value of human life. This is why most societies exact maximum punishment for wanton killing. Such criminality strikes us as monstrous because it attacks the highest value we know of. Moreover, since the perpetrator of such a crime is himself a beneficiary of life, it strikes us as the height of injustice and perversity for him to destroy other lives. The depth of moral evil that murder brings about is, therefore, fittingly characterizable by the religious notion of sin. The concept of sin carries with it the notion of perverting the original calling of man, which is to serve life and to enjoy its blessings. A greater sin it is difficult to imagine.

There is another respect in which we can condemn such a sin. A killer does evil to himself as well as to his victim. He diminishes the possibilities of his own destiny in a drastic way. To be a human being is to be a part of a larger stream, to be a bearer and beneficiary of the accumulated values and forms of existence. Each human destiny carries a stamp of the whole of mankind. Thus a murder is a repudiation, a turning against one's own essential heritage, a betrayal of one's own nature. A murder is bound to leave deep psychic scars on its perpetrator. What we call a hardened criminal is a person whose conscience has been irreparably scarred. There is a deep gulf between him and other human beings. Killing brutalizes—in the literal sense of the word.

So does war, an institutionalized form of killing. It also stands condemned by the same standard. War eliminates human destinies wholesale. Although in some situations the legitimate motive of self-defense and self-preservation may be rightly appealed to, every aggressive war is evil, whatever its professed objective. To treat human destinies as a means to an end, no matter how "hallowed" that end, is a crime, a sin. The rationalizations for such a war, when scrutinized morally, are likely to sound hollow. Each human destiny is an end in itself in the sense that each person has a right to his life and to the unhindered pursuit of his well-being. No one has the right to destroy it, even for the sake of high ideals, for these ideals cannot be as high as the value that is sacrificed to attain them.

## Participation and Evil

Besides murder there are many other forms of criminal behavior. Even though they fall short of depriving a victim of his life, by maiming or injuring him in some other way they may do serious damage to his natural capacity to participate in activities and pursuits that make life satisfying. Inflicting bodily injury, restraining free movement, stealing or destroying property, causing violence and insecurity—all these deny or diminish the possibility of relating harmoniously and fruitfully to one's physical and social surroundings. Persons who perpetrate such acts do evil, especially when these acts are performed in full knowledge of their consequences. In many instances there are mitigating or excusing circumstances. Harmful behavior often flows from plain ignorance, and in these kinds of cases the imputation of evil intent becomes, of course, problematic.

Attributing evil is especially troublesome when the evil produced has a long-range effect or is institutionally mediated. Mankind acquiesced for a long time—and still does to a great extent today—in social injustices of various forms. By allowing great discrepancies in wealth and privileges, a society is bound to truncate life's possibilities for many of its members. With a minimum of resources at their disposal, the poor have been and are the wretched of this earth, condemned to lowering their sights and to being perpetually and exclusively preoccupied with the struggle for survival. Moral and political reforms have played an important role in the history of mankind, but, alas, not always successfully.

The ideal of human brotherhood and equality is inimical to any sort of exclusiveness, however based—on racial prejudice, religious tolerance, or economic exploitation. As long as artificial barriers exist between social classes or between nations, the full benefits of participating in the experience of others are denied. Unfortunately, mankind still has not rid itself of all the evils of racism or nationalism, which pit against one another human beings who would soon learn to understand, accept, and appreciate one another if they were left to their own devices. Our epoch is still infected with this form of evil, a complicated mixture of ideological, nationalistic, and social struggles. Many human destinies are being tragically affected by the evils resulting from these struggles, which, to make matters worse, nowadays take place under the shadow of the threat of a nuclear war—the most horrible evil that ever threatened the human race. The true nature of this evil dawns on us when, instead of thinking of body counts, we try to envisage the countless person-worlds lost to the universe, each destroyed human destiny constituting such a world. Destruction on this scale would be a monstrous, unforgivable, and unredeemable sin, unforgivable and unredeemable in the literal sense, for with the destruction of mankind there would be no one, no consciousness, to forgive or to redeem.

Short of such an ultimate catastrophe there are other evils to cope with, less dramatic but nonetheless serious. I mean the absence of respect for our home: the earth and its resources. Only recently has the growing ecological concern helped us to uncover and focus on various ways we have been poisoning our environment and wastefully destroying vital resources. Here, too, the battle is likely to be prolonged and difficult because the forms of this evil are complex and intertwined—selfishness, shortsightedness, greed, fear, jostling for power, and plain ignorance. No quick solutions can be expected, and new unpleasant surprises lurk behind every corner. But, as must also be granted, mankind's experience does not exclude a modicum of good sense and goodwill, a desire to compensate for defects and deficiencies by some idealism and practical imagination. To succumb to the gospel of gloom and doom, to declare the forces of evil insuperable, is once more to fail to do justice to all the factors of human existence. A more realistic appraisal will recognize that evils can be seen *as* evils only by a consciousness that sees them against the background of a potential and desirable good.

## Compensation and Evil

The world, for us, *is* as it is experienced, and it is experienced by particular persons. Each human destiny has a unique, irreplaceable status. This belief is an intrinsic part of most world religions that proclaim the ultimate worth of every single soul. What is evil, with regard to this truth? Evil is willful interference with each person's natural desire to use his talents and to fulfill his hopes and aspirations. Evil is intolerance and hostile tampering with the development and blossoming of each human destiny in the light of its ultimate beliefs. In short, evil is an illegitimate arrogation of the power to decide what the universe, as expressed in the life and thought of an individual, should be. To play with another person's life is to play God, or at least the Grand Inquisitor. This is why all forms of suppression of individual conscience, all blocking of creativity, all deliberate stunting of personal growth, are forms of evil.

A society that relies on coercion and terror to deprive its members of the right to seek fulfillment of their own destinies in the light of freely acquired values and convictions, no matter how good its intentions may be, unwittingly undermines these intentions. The well-being of future generations cannot be improved if in the process of trying to improve it the life of the present generation is twisted and stunted. Deprived of the opportunity to think for themselves, to arrive at their own conclusions, to share and compare freely views and opinions, people are bound to acquire psychic scars that distort their consciousnesses and consciences.

The preservation of each individual's freedom to live his life in his own way is a religious imperative. Of course this injunction has obvious limits: where the individual's actions infringe on equal rights of others, appropriate sanctions are justified. The determination of such limits is not an easy matter. It has been the subject of a lengthy debate throughout human history, and we still do not know precisely what kind of social order and what kind of political and economic institutions would be most successful in securing both individual and social rights. In this area optimum solutions have not been reached, although it is possible to identify societies that on the whole have managed to strike the right balance. But at least we know what evils are to be guarded against in this area because we know what values are at stake.

Evil, whatever its form, can come about either deliberately or inadvertently, often because of ignorance. On the whole, the sins of commission present a more blatant form of evil. Willful evil must be opposed whenever it appears. Evils due to omission or ignorance are a different matter. Although mercy-seasoned justice is always commendable, it is especially in order if the evil of our actions arises from complex motives, for half-understood reasons, and out of inadequate knowledge. This points to the importance of enlarging our awareness and improving our education. Where evil is concerned, that education should be definitely of a moral sort. Moral learning is a complex affair; it involves not only the conditioning of the will but also the education of emotions. It awakens our wider sympathies and introduces gentleness into our souls. Respect for human life will have a stronger hold on a person if that person has been encouraged to love and to respond to all surrounding life from early childhood. The path away from evil leads to a greater sensitivity and appreciation of all creation. The recognition of special gifts in the human species need not close our eyes to the fact that the universe celebrates itself in other forms of consciousness—no matter how partial or rudimentary. It is not difficult to perceive the life-affirming forces of the universe breaking through in the *joi de vivre* of a playing kitten, a soaring seagull, or a leaping gazelle. Although a person's gentler feelings and wider sympathies may be often drowned or distorted by harsh or fortuitous events in later life, the cultivation of such feelings and sympathies in a child and their strengthening and development in further education may help diminish the appeal of evil.

## NOTES

[1]George Eliot, *Scenes of Clerical Life*, (Boston and New York: Houghton Mifflin, 1907), p. 179.

CHAPTER 4

# Meaning

## "Meaning" in the "Meaning of Life"

The discussion of the preceding chapters should alert us to a special feature of the question, "What is the meaning of life?" When we ask this question, we do not inquire about the meaning of the word *life*. Already as children we learn to distinguish living from nonliving or dead things, so that distinction is not the target of our question. It is also quite clear that in asking about the meaning of life we are not asking about *all* life; we mean to exclude other animals and the entire realm of nonanimal life. In other words, the question is usually confined to *human* life.

Closer attention to the typical context in which this

question is earnestly asked will reveal that its target con-
tracts even further. The person asking whether life has
meaning wants to determine whether *his* or *her* life has
meaning. He or she is not engaged in an abstract musing
about the general phenomenon of life on earth or about
mankind as a whole. The ultimate target of this question is
oneself. The reference to other human beings or to other
forms of life or to the history of the cosmos is relevant only
when it helps to answer the question, "Does my life have
meaning?" The interest in phenomena other than one's
own life is important only as it has a bearing on that question. If this is so, then the question becomes essentially,
"Does *my* life have meaning?"

An answer to this question must be based on the experience of the person asking it since the ultimate ground on
which this question can be answered is personal experience.
A peculiar feature of this question is that it cannot be asked
abstractly or generally without reference to the subjectivity
of the person asking it. Indeed, the very asking of the question calls for a personal verdict. I cannot ask this question
while remaining indifferent to what that verdict might be.
Even if my answer to this question is "Nothing matters, my
life included," I cannot escape the consequences of this
judgment.

I can experience whatever values the universe has to
offer only as *my* values. Although this is a universal truth,
applicable to all persons, the concrete embodiment or ver-
ification of this truth will happen only in my life. No one can
discover for me what meaning life has. Unless I find the
meaning of life in my life, it will forever escape me. I have
only one life to live, and no one can live it for me. Whatever
the meaning of the universe or the cosmos is, that meaning
is accessible to me only through my life's experience. This

proposition is also a universal truth, applicable to any person. Whatever I may learn about the universe from physics, from chemistry, astronomy, geology, or biology; whatever I may learn about the experience of the human race through the study of anthropology, history, or sociology; whatever I may appreciate as creations of the human spirit in science or in art—all of these forms of awareness will be appropriated by me as conscious, active, evaluating agents.

There is a possibility that this conclusion will be misunderstood as leading to a position for which philosophers have invented a special name: solipsism. Solipsism is a belief that when a person begins to analyze what is available to him in experience he is bound to conclude that he is the only existing reality. Many thinkers have discovered something seductive about this train of thought: it is difficult to escape the solipsistic conclusion if one accepts certain initial premises. The philosophies of such illustrious thinkers as René Descartes and George Berkeley run this danger, and some contemporary thought is also not immune to it. Unexpectedly and surprisingly one may find oneself boxed into a telephone booth with no wires leading from it. A closer examination of solipsism seems desirable to make clear that this philosophical position does not follow from the view advocated in this essay, though it may contain a germ of an important truth.

## Meaning and Solipsism

A certain train of thought seems to lead irresistibly to the conclusion that I am the only existing reality. The argument is very simple. Everything that I am aware of presents itself to me as a form of my consciousness. The very attempt to speak of confronting something other than my experience is incoherent, for if there is some reality outside my experience, then that reality can be accessible to me only in some mode of my awareness. If there is something that strikes me, I cannot know it in itself, for I can be aware of it only through the event of its striking me, and *this* takes place in me; it has to be some form of my experience, not something "outside" of it.

When John Locke distinguished between primary and secondary qualities of objects, he claimed that the ideas of the latter, that is, of particular colors, tastes, and sounds, do not exist in the objects but only in the minds of the perceivers. In contrast, the primary qualities, such as size and shape, Locke thought to be independent of the way in which we perceive them. But as George Berkeley pointed out later, I cannot know whether the so-called primary qualities exist independently of my mind because what is available to me in experience is only my *perception* of these qualities, not the qualities themselves.

*My* world, then, *is* as it appears to me, and there is nothing independent of the sum total of these appearances. This conclusion is not in any way affected by adopting the scientific attitude, which presents the composition and the behavior of physical objects and phenomena in theoretical terms. When I view the world theoretically, I merely am enriching my perceptions by elaborate frameworks of conceptual relationships. The awareness of these relationships is still *my* awareness, and when it allegedly touches an independent reality at points of experimental data or verifications, these data and verifications are also no more than my perceptions.

The solipsistic conclusion is not undermined when I include the reality of other people in my experience. My

contact with other people also consists of having perceptions, sensations, and thoughts of various sorts. Even when
I consult others to try to assure myself that I really perceive
something and am not a victim of a delusion or a hallucina-
tion, the opinions and assurances I hear are an integral part
of my experience. The existence and the activity of others
manifest themselves either on the screen of my mind or not
at all. The fact that my perceptions usually agree with those
of others need not be explained by postulating an independent existence of those others. After all, I know the others
only to the extent that they affect or impinge on my
experience.

The order revealed in my perceptions and in my
dealing with others need not be ascribed to the operation or
activity of any external agency. That my experience hangs
together, exhibits a high degree of order and regularity, and
enables me to make correct predictions of what I am to
expect in the way of further occurrences is something inter-
nal to my experience. There is no reason why solipsism
should be conceptually married to chaos. It is simply a fact
that my experience exhibits a high degree of order, and this
fact cannot be explained by postulating something outside
this order because there is simply no way of *getting* outside
that order. My world is my experience.

In spite of its apparent plausibility when pursued along
the lines just suggested, the argument for solipsism pro-
duces no conviction. It goes against the grain of the irresistible belief that I am confronted by an independently existing
real world that includes other human beings as well. This
conviction grows out of countless encounters with immov-
able objects that stubbornly and implacably block my path
in spite of my frequent desire to have them out of my way.
Objective reality stares me in the face and inevitably stares

me down; there is no contest. I am not just dreaming my world. Even if I am inclined to theorize that the distinction between dream and reality is a distinction that exists only within my experience, the theory founders on the fact that while dreams vanish into thin air when I wake up, objective reality exhibits no such tendency. No matter how ardently I may wish for things to be different, they persist. They have no respect for my wishes.

A purely logical argument can also be used to undermine solipsism. It has been used in an illuminating way by Ludwig Wittgenstein. When I ask myself how I can assign meaning to my experience, I notice that that meaning arises as a result of characterizing my perceptions, observations, or sensations. To do this I need words—language. To characterize a color as red, I must understand the word *red* or have a concept of redness. How do I come to understand the concept or to learn the word? I certainly do not get it out of thin air, out of contemplating a bit of my private experience. The simple truth is that I have learned the word *from other people*—parents or teachers. They showed me and told me which things are called red. They corrected me when I made mistakes. They taught me *under what circumstances* it is correct to use the word. So in the very process of learning how to characterize my supposedly solipsistic world, I was being affected by others all along. Moreover, the members of my linguistic community and I were not merely comparing the contents of our minds when teaching concepts to one another. We needed to refer to surrounding circumstances, to facts that warranted the use of certain words and locutions. In the presence of these circumstances we discovered that we can and do agree in our characterizations of experiences, that is, that we share a *common* world.

The very possibility of language depends on common responses by other beings to the persisting features of the world. Our ability to use words to identify colors, to engage in the activities of pointing to, sorting out, and distinguishing particular objects and their characteristics, can be experienced as a remarkable fact about ourselves and the world. Something *is* being shared when one person exclaims to another, "Look, how blue the sky is today!" He is certainly not pointing to private inner sensations and then somehow realizing that these sensations are the same or similar. He is referring to the sky and its blueness. In doing so he manifests something special about human experience, namely, the capacity to recognize the presence of a common world. Of course, that world is not merely "out there" in splendid isolation. That world is *shared*; it is responded to in the same way by different individuals. So at the very outset the question of the independence or complete transcendence of the "real world" answers itself. Perception is not subjective, i.e., present only in the eyes or the mind of the beholder; it is independent of him in the sense that sometimes he can be shown to be wrong or be corrected by others. On the other hand, that which makes perception veridical is the fact that people agree in their judgments about the ways the perceived objects strike them—in the way of color, or shape, or taste, or the emitted sound.

While I reflect on this argument, I notice that I could not invent a "private language," language that only I could understand. The reason for this is that if I wanted to identify certain perceptions or sensations in that supposed language, I would lack any assurance that I used that language correctly. Suppose I characterize an experience I am having now as the same experience I had yesterday. I think that because, I have called $E$ yesterday, the experience, I am entitled to call it *E* today. But what entitles me to think that I am correct, that I am not mistaken? What I have is merely the memory of yesterday's experience. How do I know that this memory is correct? Could anything show that it is incorrect? Ordinarily, when we use (public) language, we can question whether we remember something correctly. We may check the memory claim against the circumstances (including the memories of other people), and if the circumstances do not bear out the claim, we withdraw the claim and admit that the memory was incorrect, that we merely thought that we remembered, but did not.

In the case of private language there is no recourse to checking against the circumstances because such checking cannot make use of publicly acknowledged characterizations—all characterizations are private, my own. But this means that I cannot distinguish between what I seem to remember and what I really remember. So when I call today's experience *E* on the basis of such a "memory," I cannot call it right, regard it as correct. What seems right is right. And this means that I cannot communicate my experience successfully in such a private language.

Instead, in real life I always make use of public language with common meanings. This reliance means that my experience does not arise out of my own inner resources but begins with the encounter of real things characterized for me by other people.

To ask for the meaning of a word is to ask for its place in the conceptual framework of a given linguistic community. In the use of language there emerges a conception of a common world in which particular objects, rules, and practices are parts or components. I understand what a word means or how a concept is used because I have been taught that meaning or that use by others. Thus, I do not stand alone. Solipsism is refuted.

## Meaning through Personal Evaluation

Having rejected solipsism as untenable, we return to the claim that the question "Does life have meaning?" in actuality is equivalent to asking "Does *my* life have meaning?" What is the point of this claim? Its point is that there is something right about the solipsistic stance, provided it is properly circumscribed. What is right about it perhaps could be labeled "valuational solipsism." Let us see what can be said in the way of justifying the use of this phrase.

We have noted that a serious reflection on the meaning of life presents the inquirer with his own life as the datum on which he must base his conclusions. Here it may be worth recalling A. N. Whitehead's words when he declared that religion is what each man does with his solitariness. There is much truth in these words. If I am to discover life's meaning, I must discover it in my life. But isn't this a mere truism? Yes, but it is a crucially important one. The difficulty lies, paradoxically, in seeing how simple and inescapable it is. It calls attention to the fact that the quest for meaning is a personal task. Unless *I* find meaning in the universe, it will not be found, as far as I am concerned. This is true for every other person as well.

The use of "meaning" in this connection is logically incomplete without presupposing a consciousness to whom the meaning is apparent. Meaning here is conceived in a valuational sense. In this sense the logical implication of the search for meaning is that *if* meaning is found, it will be apparent to the person searching for it. Whatever the verdict on the question, that verdict—positive or negative—must be acknowledged by the person asking it.

To speak of the meaning *of the universe* is to speak of the way this meaning becomes apparent in personal experience. This is the only way the universe can manifest meaning. Indeed, even to imagine the universe as having meaning apart from particular conscious lives is to personalize the universe, to make it a locus of consciousness, or to regard it as governed by some higher consciousness. The history of human thought contains many examples of attempts to think of the universe as a living, conscious being; pantheistic or panpsychistic visions have had a recurrent attraction for most serious thinkers. The main difficulty with all of them is that they are so obviously anthropomorphic, no matter whether the all-encompassing Being is called God or Om or the One. When such pictures are not crudely anthropomorphic and are meant to be merely analogical, the analogies are either difficult to draw or difficult to sustain.

We need not be detained by thorny metaphysical or theological questions surrounding such pictures. For our purposes it is sufficient to realize that even if such imaginary constructions could be shown to have a foothold in reality, the general view defended here still would hold—with one modification. In addition to finite, particular centers of experience, there also would be an infinite one that obviously would have an all-inclusive perspective. It would be *a* perspective, from God's, or the Absolute's, point of view. What is important is that such a perspective would include a valuational judgment (for example, God proclaiming the world good upon creating it or judging it to be wicked and deserving punishment).

The reference to God's judgment, decision, and action calls attention to a connection between valuational solipsism and freedom. As a finite center of experience I too am called to judge, decide, and act. My understanding of what is valuable helps shape my individual career. Here lies the importance of the question about the meaning of life. Since I am to judge how life appears to me or how I understand it, I will use my knowledge and my opportunities in the light of this judgment. My picture of the world differs in some respects from the picture even of those with whom I share a common world and, on the whole, agree about basic realities, both natural and human. To say the least, my fantasies are peculiar to me; so are my dreams and what I make of them. Of course, I may get help on this most intimate aspect of my experience from an expert, a psychiatrist. But even he needs to be told *by me* what my dreams are before he can suggest deeper interpretations. The world of imagination, however, is but a fraction of what constitutes my thoughts, my opinions, my personal purposes and evaluations. With obvious and important reservations, there is no denying that my world, understood as the meaning of my experience, is what I judge it to be.

The realization of the truth of valuational solipsism should have important psychological consequences. Whether the universe has meaning or not can be answered, as we have seen, only in the light of my own experience—I cannot find it anywhere else. This goes for every person. Therefore, we are justified in saying that each human being reflects the meaning of the universe. Each of us pronounces the verdict on that meaning as it comes to life and light in our individual consciousnesses. The meaning I find discloses what the universe, in and through me, is—valuationally conceived. A deeper thought behind this discovery is that the universe *requires us* if that meaning is to be realized. It is not farfetched to say that our joys and celebrations are the way the universe celebrates itself. As far as we know, it is the only way in which it *can* celebrate itself, namely, in the consciousness of individuals. The same is true for disvalues, for only where values can be realized are disvalues possible. Whether I rejoice or mourn, my life is the gate through which rejoicing and mourning surface in the cosmos.

The reference to the value-disvalue dialectic should serve as a corrective to the pessimism of some doctrines captured in such sayings as, "I am alone and afraid in the world I never made." Such observations and many traditional proverbs have an overtone of sadness, despair, isolation. But even these moods bring out the truth of valuational solipsism: the *negative* verdict on the meaning and value of human life also emerges from individual centers of consciousness. There is no denial that such pessimistic verdicts often appear justified. Nevertheless, it would be folly not to acknowledge occurrences of joy, pleasure, celebration, and fulfillment. To the extent that *they* enter my life I have cause to declare the universe a success, to say yes and amen to it. The fact of human finitude cannot be invoked as justifying an ultimately negative verdict on human life. As we have seen in the first chapter, the general condemnation of life simply on account of its finitude is due to a misleading picture of life as inevitably married to such unhelpful dialectical contrasts as finitude-infinitude, life-death, time-eternity. Valuational solipsism underscores the notion that everyone of us is charged with transforming his or her life into a destiny.

The idea of destiny, then, constitutes the conceptual core of the entire view presented here. The central message of this view is that the target of the quest for meaning is primarily onself and one's experience. But this is a far cry from solipsism. Chapter 2 (Participation) attempted to show that the opposite of solipsism is actually true: each individual destiny lives, moves, and has its being in an objective world that has multiple dimensions. The chapter on compensation rounded out our discussion by reminding us that the recognition and appreciation of personally experienced values has a bearing on whether the universe has meaning or not. In this way the idea of compensation illumines the connection between the perennial religious quest and the universal human search for meaning.

# Epilogue

Absorbing new insights and translating them into stable, dominant attitudes is a matter of use, of cultivation. This is true about the central claims of this essay as well. To be firmly imprinted on one's mind they require an effort of assimilation and habituation. If they are to become truly effective in practice, they must be constantly reevaluated as they are applied to various life situations. We need to remind ourselves of their relevance on frequent occasions. Otherwise, like all other truths and insights, they may become dissolved and dissipated by the pressures of immediate concerns.

When daily concerns are especially pressing and even depressing, it is important to *create a space* for an exercise of what we have called solipsistic valuation. All too often the weight of the world may appear overwhelming, depriving us of all capacity for freedom, initiative, and enjoyment. At such times we tend to assign all value to events going on outside of ourselves. We feel the world to be "an implacable force brooding over an inscrutable intention." But there is no such force and no such intention; to think so is to fall victim to the pathetic fallacy. There are only other people, caught up in *their* intentions, projects, destinies, some of which are sometimes at cross-purposes with ours.

Nothing seems more appropriate, more wholesome, more healing than an effort to incorporate the trying, difficult moment into the depths of our destiny. When we view adversity as a fragment of a larger whole and direct our attention and emotion to that larger whole, we may be liberated from the imprisonment of the flat surface of our vision. Such an adjustment will remove our enslavement to the dimensionless point and will enable us to adopt a point of view, to see our situation from a perspective. The painful moment will not necessarily cease being painful, but its darkness may be softened by the surrounding light.

This train of thought should remind us once more of the central thesis of this essay. There is no meaningful reality apart from human reality, and the only access to that reality is through individual personal experience. The last phrase is really a pleonasm, because all experience is individual and personal. Experience is always *some person's* experience. Each one of us is a center, a bearer of meaning that lights up the universe and makes *it* meaningful. To impute egotism to this view is to misunderstand it fundamentally. Egotism minimizes or plays down the importance of others; our view finds everyone's experience equally important. But it reminds us, nevertheless, that each person's destiny is a unique and irreplaceable realization of values that the scheme of things reveals. Each one of us is a center in which the value, the meaning of the universe, becomes a concrete reality. This affirmation of radical humanism, of the ultimate importance of each human person, should furnish the basis for two constant reminders.

First, the present moment is the center from which and to which my destiny radiates. All reality, for me, is the present time and place. The stranger in Albert Camus's novel concluded that every human being is privileged. This observation should be extended by adding that each moment of a human life is privileged. My joys and my sorrows are the ways in which the universe experiences itself through me. Each moment of my life is a focal point of a larger sweep of my destiny, encompassing all its interconnections in ever-growing concentric circles. Hence, I should see each moment as belonging to this totality, to this unique, unrepeatable manifestation of the universe.

Two, in meeting a person I meet a world; I am brought face to face with another singular and unrepeatable manifestation of cosmic meaning. But in sharing a language, knowledge, customs, rituals, projects, and other activities of life with my fellow men, I may enter these worlds, and they may enter mine. Moreover, such sharing is not restricted to actual interactions of my lifetime. On some occasions I may become aware of the extent to which my life soaks up and is enriched by the achievements of many other human beings, living or dead. This happens when I am moved by some specific acts or creations of the human spirit. In this way the content of other lives, even those remote in time and space, may become mine. When the unique worlds touch one another deeply, they may become united in a dimension that deserves to be called religious.

People need other people. We need each other in times of stress, and we need each other in times of joy—to seek help, to share happiness. But there may be even those extreme situations when one's whole life seems empty and irrelevant—we do get bored with ourselves. And this is precisely the time to become a harmless parasite by feeding on the meaning of other people's lives. Are you bored with yourself? Well, don't despair; this happens even to the most scintillating personalities. But with luck, by a dint of curiosity coupled with a dash of empathy, we may get the vicarious satisfaction of becoming interested, or wondering, or amused, or surprised, or perhaps on some occasions even uplifted spectators of other destinies. We are told that many a parent or a lover, having lost all zest for living, nevertheless retains a sense of purposive existence by living for others. (This has its dangers. There was, they say, a lady in Aberdeen who lived for others, and you can tell who those others were by their haunted looks.)

But even in more transient, mundane moods of temporary ennui, there is a remedy. We may be vicarious, sympathetic participants in the life drama around us. Perhaps this is one possible meaning of the saying that he who loses his soul shall find it.

Religiousness, in our extended sense of the word, can permeate all of our experience; it can be relevant today and every day. This suggestion appears to be in conflict with a basic distinction between the profane and the sacred, the natural and the supernatural; most religions insist on this distinction. Yet most religions also enjoin believers to follow the precepts of religion in daily living. Somehow there appears to be a conflict here. If the sacred is on an altogether different plane from the profane, then their union is problematic. Not surprisingly, theologians try to make plausible the notion of special religious experiences that can "reveal" the sacred to the believer. Contrasted with the sacred, all other experiences proceed on the ordinary, profane plane, rendering unto Caesar that which is Caesar's. Although something of the religious vision is supposed to carry over from the peaks of experience to its valleys, in actual practice, in the bustle of daily living, the sacred plane disappears from sight—it is not even seen, in the Bible phrase, as if through glass, darkly.

The drift of the view developed in these pages is that we should resist the distinction between the profane and the sacred. That distinction makes the application and relevance of religion to life problematic. If we are to recover the sense of the meaning of life, we must discover it *in* life, not in a special realm outside of it. I have concluded that a certain way of regarding our own lives and the lives of others may generate an attitude that deserves to be called religious. Perhaps I can elaborate on this conclusion once more by constructing additional conceptual pictures that may have practical application in daily living.

Religiousness calls for keeping in an active balance two countermotions of the soul: centripetal and centrifugal. I am borrowing unashamedly these notions from classical physics because, first, they are a fitting vehicle for a summary presentation of the entire conceptual scheme of this essay; and, second, they may be useful as a simple mnemonic device to see the applicability of this scheme to a religious conception of life.

First, we ought to give free rein the centripetal motion of our souls in order to develop the habit of seeing ourselves *as a destiny,* as individual centers of experience through which the universe gets to know itself. It is important to encourage this motion to remain actively in force because of the distracting influences of the surrounding world. The world should claim our attention; it will do so in any case, but we should resist the tacit suggestion or insinuation that "the real show" goes on *elsewhere*—in some other place or at some other time—and that, compared to that show, our experience is secondary or unimportant. The truth in solipsism is a healthy corrective to this delusion. According to Giordano Bruno, the real discovery behind the Copernican revolution was that the universe has no center. A further corollary of Bruno's observation is that *any* point of the universe can be regarded as its center. Each human destiny *is* analogously such a center.

Consider the phenomenon of being the object of someone's love. Being loved by another person—a parent, a lover—is probably the best analog to being the center of the universe. An intense, deep love is a concrete recognition of the uniqueness of a destiny and its value. In this light, it is not surprising that, according to Christians, God loves every person unconditionally. We come closest to experiencing ultimate values by being the object of deep, abiding love. The desirability of being loved is, or may be, another matter. Yet in the most desirable experiences we know of— being the focus of someone's love—the central importance of individual human destinies is evident.

The second motion of the soul is centrifugal. Its nature can also be discerned in the illustration just cited. To be able to love someone is not any less valuable to us than being loved. The experience of being in love is a perfect example of participation. Loving—taking an interest in, being devoted to—another is a way of moving from the center of one's own being to the being of others. Participation is a far-flung and open-ended affair. It involves joining all kinds of activities: intellectual and artistic, social and political, theoretical and practical. It gives content to our destinies by connecting them with their immediate and mediate surroundings, both natural and human. To enlarge my sympathies and understanding, to play a role in the unfolding of mankind's experience, is to enrich my destiny. Thus the centrifugal motion of the soul, not restricted to loving one's neighbor, is a phenomenon of religiousness, concomitant to the centripetal appreciation of my own destiny.

Another picture may be invoked to clarify the conception of destiny developed in this essay. Think of each moment of life as gathering into itself the rays of its heritage and influence. The focus of this gathering has both a horizontal and a vertical axis. The horizontal axis is the axis of participation; it traces the connections with the past, through the present, with the future. The vertical axis traces the individual path of a human career as it is lived and as it gains depth and height. The line of the melody is enhanced by the counterpoint of harmony. Both distinctions, the centrifugal-centripetal and the horizontal-vertical, may help us to view human experience as a system in which two converging forces are in active balance. Both my inner-directedness and my world-directedness are acts of consciousness that take place in time. Since I see myself and others as such systems, I should not regard either myself or others as momentary states, but always as destinies, as careers in development. This may enable me to see myself and others with greater tolerance and forebearance, with a concern for the long-term well-being of every person.

All too frequently, perhaps most of the time, we "take in" only the proximate, momentarily available, aspects of people with whom we are in contact. (This is not really surprising, because most of the time we tend to have such a fragmented, short-range, immediate project-oriented view even of our own selves.) But this is myopic. We should train ourselves to "keep in view" the larger segments of human destinies around us. We usually focus our attention on the whole of a person's career only when he dies. Thinking of a deceased relative or friend, we may formulate a sort of vague epitaph, a summary, an homage. But why wait until a person dies to regard his person in a more inclusive, more comprehensive fashion? Why not form epitaphs for the living, not as marking our regret, grief, or sorrow, but as indicating awareness, and possibly appreciation, of the wholeness or totality that at each moment lives, moves, and has its being under the pulsating surface. It is not likely that we can ever *sum up* a person as a total project—not even in our own case. But we may be more fair, more understanding, more fully in contact with others if we try to see them always as *whole* persons—finite, but unique and unrepeatable.

Each system, or each destiny, is of course a *differentiated* whole. Not every occasion of life reveals something representative of our total self. Similarly, opportunities for self-knowledge and reflection do not come very often. Obviously, moments of relative repose free from immediate concerns are more likely to make me aware of the nature of my ultimate situation, of the course of my destiny and participation, and of the various forms in which compensation can counterbalance my finitude. In that regard, the view of religiousness defended in this essay is not inimical to the benefits of meditation, withdrawal, and solitude. On the contrary, since this view encourages the full use of all the powers of the mind, such activities will form a part of the good life, in addition to a more straightforwardly intellectual effort, without which even the reading of this (or any other) essay cannot bear fruit.

Let me conclude by returning to the thought expressed in the first paragraph of this epilogue: nothing comes without effort. We will not find meaning in our lives if we do not *try* to see it. But, to be realistic, we must be also modest; we must not set our sights too high. No one can or should live constantly at the level of deep introspection. The world is too much with us for this to be possible. But we need to retreat within the narrower confines of our being in order to feel its depths and canvass its horizons. We must *take* time to muse a bit about our place in the total scheme of things. Such musement may lead us to the discovery that our destinies matter. Indeed, the main point of this essay is to show that *the world* matters only because each human life, yours and mine, matters first of all. It matters in the isolation of our private destinies, in our participation in the destinies of others, and in the compensatory efforts of our minds and hearts, which redeem and justify our finitude.

DATE DUE